New Ways in Teaching English at the Secondary Level

Deborah J. Short, Editor

New Ways in TESOL Series II
Innovative Classroom Techniques
Jack C. Richards, Series Editor

TESOL
Founded 1966

Teachers of English to Speakers of Other Languages, Inc.

Typeset in Garamond Book and Tiffany Demi
by Capitol Communication Systems, Inc. Crofton, Maryland USA
and printed by Pantagraph Printing, Bloomington, Illinois USA

Teachers of English to Speakers of Other Languages, Inc.
1600 Cameron Street, Suite 300
Alexandria, Virginia 22314 USA
Tel 703-836-0774 • Fax 703-836-7864 • E-mail publ@tesol.edu • http://www.tesol.edu/

Director of Communications and Marketing: Helen Kornblum
Managing Editor: Marilyn Kupetz
Copy Editor: Christa Watters
Cover Design: Ann Kammerer

ISBN 0-939-791-77-3
Library of Congress Catalog No. 98-061415

Dedication

To my father, John M. Short, the first secondary language teacher I knew and a continuing model for me.

Contents

Acknowledgments

I would like to thank all the ESL and EFL teachers who contributed their thoughtful and creative ideas for this volume on teaching English to secondary-level students. It is their techniques that will make this book useful to ESL and EFL teachers worldwide.

I would like to acknowledge the support of Donna Christian, president of the Center for Applied Linguistics (CAL), and the assistance of my colleagues at CAL: Annette Holmes, Margaret Crandall, Quang Pho, Michaell Myrie, and Ming Pho. Their help with keyboarding, graphics, decoding files, and managing Internet transfers was invaluable.

Thanks are also extended to Helen Kornblum, director of Communications and Marketing, and Marilyn Kupetz, managing editor, at the TESOL Central Office for their guidance and patience. Jack Richards and David Nunan, former chairs of the TESOL Publication Committee, have been supportive as well.

Introduction

This book offers an international collection of best practices that address the particular interests and demands of working at the secondary level in both ESL and EFL settings. Created by ESL and EFL colleagues who teach at the secondary level, the activities included here are classroom tested and student approved. Unlike some earlier books in the New Ways series, this volume does not focus on a single language skill (e.g., listening). Rather, it compiles a series of integrated activities that mirror more closely the type of teaching we do in our secondary classrooms, where we combine all the skills and features of language learning.

The contributions to this book are creative and versatile, with a range of activities involving authentic literature, academic content, multimedia use, peer cooperation, career information, and more. The authors have described the steps for the activities carefully, and many have included handouts and other resource material to facilitate use in the classroom. The contributors have also indicated where in a lesson they might use the techniques—as a motivator, for practice or application, or as an assessment. Some contributions describe projects that may be done by individual students, by the class, or in collaboration with another class. You will see as you peruse the collection that most of the techniques have several objectives, as is common in secondary classrooms. Along with a speaking activity, for instance, students practice note-taking; or reading and writing are combined with summarizing and illustrating. One key ingredient to all these activities is academic preparation for the students. All the authors acknowledge the need for the students to be successful in the course work at the secondary level. Whether the students are studying English as a second or foreign language, the academic skills they learn and practice through their language course will serve them well in other school subjects.

The book is divided into several main sections: Icebreakers to Start the School Year; Integrated Language Development Activities; Connections with Content Areas; Multimedia Infusion; Cooperative Projects; and Assessment, Review, and Language Games. Several sections are subdivided to organize the contributions further.

The format for each of the contributions is the same. This user-friendly style should help you glance through the activities quickly to understand the goals and procedures. The setting for the activity is provided: English proficiency level, school level (as appropriate[1]), aims for student learning, type of activity (e.g., motivation, practice, review), time needed for preparation and implementation, and required resources. Then the procedures are written in steps and are followed by a caveats and options section where the authors call attention to other uses of the activity and describe adaptations that can be made. For those with handouts or graphics, an appendix accompanies the contribution.

With this new book, we will have a resource specifically designed for our needs at the secondary level, generated by ourselves and our colleagues, offering a worldwide perspective on language teaching. The collection of activities captures, in a concise manner, the holistic picture of what we do in our secondary classrooms, based on first-hand experience of language professionals. I hope you will find it useful and be eager to take these new techniques into your own classroom.

[1]The school levels are based on the U.S. school system. Middle school is similar to junior high and usually serves students 11–14 years old. High school usually serves students 14–18 years old, although most schools allow students to remain until age 21 to get a diploma. If there is no school-level designation, the activity is appropriate for all secondary students.

Users' Guide to Activities

Developing Language Through Writing

Part III: Connections With Content Areas

Integrating Language With Academic Content

Part V: Cooperative Projects

Part VI: Assessment, Review, and Language Games

Part I: Icebreakers to Start the School Year

Editor's Note

This section includes activities that help students get to know one another and become familiar with the school and resources within it. The first set of activities, "Getting to Know Your Classmates," focuses on the students. Through enjoyable games and conversational tasks, students learn about others in their class or in other classes that pair up with them. Most of these activities also help students practice speaking and listening in English and develop team building skills. The last entry in this set asks students to write and share an autobiography.

The second set of activities, "Getting to Know Your School," uses guided tours or written directions to move students to different locations in the school where they record information. Observation and writing skills are practiced while they learn about their school and the staff members in it.

◆ Getting to Know Your Classmates

Can You Run Backwards?

Levels
Beginning—
intermediate

Aims
Meet new classmates in
an informal way
Practice question
structure
Learn new vocabulary
Become acquainted
with U.S. cultural ideas
Practice listening and
speaking

Activity Type
Motivation, application,
or review

Class Time
45 minutes

Preparation Time
1 hour

Resources
Sample skills list
handout

This activity stimulates meaningful interaction and helps to break the ice at the beginning of the year. Although most students may not readily remember each other's names and country of origin, almost all will recall the student who could wiggle her ears or make ice cream.

Procedure

1. Give each student a skills list handout. (See Appendix.)
2. To prepare for the activity, preteach or review vocabulary that may be new for the students (e.g., *gin rummy, wiggle, ruckus*).
3. Ask the students to introduce themselves to each other informally and find out who can do the activities listed. Have each student write the name of the classmate(s) who can perform the skill.
4. Make sure all students stand and circulate around the room during the activity.
5. After about 20-25 minutes, ask the students to return to their seats and discuss as a class who possesses certain skills.

Caveats and Options

1. Use this activity after the first class meeting when students may introduce themselves in a formal way.
2. If some students complete the sheet with one name per skill prior to the end of the activity time (20-25 minutes), they can continue to circulate and add more names.
3. After the students share the information they have gathered, ask some of them to demonstrate their skills.

4. Upon completion of the activity and for the next class meeting, divide the students into groups of three or four. Ask the groups to create a list of activities common to their own cultures or countries. The activity can be repeated in a subsequent class meeting.

Appendix: Sample Introduction Game

Can You Run Backwards?

_____ swim underwater	_____ jump rope
_____ play the fiddle	_____ write a play
_____ stand on one leg	_____ see in the dark
_____ recite poetry	_____ deal a winning hand
_____ whistle a tune	_____ predict the future
_____ play gin rummy	_____ sleepwalk
_____ run backwards	_____ wiggle your ears
_____ make ice cream	_____ call a cab
_____ raise a ruckus	_____ paint a picture
_____ spend money	_____ carve a slingshot
_____ scrunch up your nose	_____ make fudge
_____ ride a jet ski	_____ jiggle your love handles
_____ bat your eyelashes	_____ stand on your head
_____ speak Russian	_____ sing "Happy Birthday"
_____ hold your breath	in English
for 3 minutes	_____ wink with your left eye
_____ make a mess	_____ eat spaghetti with a spoon
_____ make a _really_ funny face	

Contributor

Joyce K. Gianato holds an MEd in TESOL. She has taught ESL/EFL in Italy, England, Malta, and the United States. She currently teaches in South Korea.

Catalog Puppets

Levels
Beginning; middle
school

Aims
Learn greetings, names,
pronouns
Review vocabulary
Practice natural
speaking skills

Activity Type
Practice

Class Time
50 minutes

Preparation Time
15 minutes

Resources
Sales catalogs or
magazines
Scissors
Tag board, glue, popsicle
sticks

This activity generates student conversation and reinforces dialogue practice because students are less self-conscious about speaking when using puppets. Because students choose the figures, puppets are individualized. The figures can be used again for a variety of vocabulary topics.

Procedure

1. Distribute materials and ask students to find, in the magazines or catalogs, pictures of people that represent family, friends, well-known people, or people they would like to meet (e.g., celebrities). Ask students to cut out their choice of figures and glue them onto a piece of tag board and then onto a Popsicle stick.
2. Ask students to assign a name to each of their puppets.
3. Demonstrate the activity with the whole class, using a puppet set yourself. Have your puppet ask another puppet questions you are currently studying (e.g., "How are you?" "What is your name?" "What is his name?" "What is her name?") and go around the room letting students ask and answer you.
4. Ask students to work in pairs using similar puppet conversations with each other. Circulate, helping when needed.
5. Join pairs to forms groups of four to enlarge the speaking/listening audience.

Caveats and Options

1. Let each student make a complete family of puppets for more discussions between members of the puppet family, adding family vocabulary (e.g., *mother, father, sister, baby*). Students can select more pictures to represent extended families or friends.

2. Use these puppets when learning clothing vocabulary by discussing what each one is wearing. Students may choose to create more puppets to demonstrate more options.
3. Let students create roles for their puppets to extend conversations (e.g., *occupations, homes, cities, education*). These can be the basis for a related writing assignment.
4. For students who need more practice, continue to use these puppets.

Contributor

Joan M. Dungey has taught ESL at all levels. She is the author of numerous journal articles and a frequent presenter at TESOL conferences.

Split Second Encounters

Levels
Any

Aims
Get acquainted
Formulate questions
Practice real-life
communication
Make decisions
Initiate conversations
Practice listening and
speaking

Activity Type
Motivation or
application

Class Time
15–45 minutes

Preparation Time
30 minutes

Resources
Timer (or watch or
clock with a second
hand)
5-in. x 8-in. index cards
(one per student)
Rubber clock-face stamp
and ink pad (optional)
List of conversation
starters

For this cooperative learning activity, a Spanish class works with a predominantly Spanish-speaking ESL class. The task provides both groups the opportunity for a multicultural exchange and stimulates conversation in a real-life situation.

Procedure

1. In advance of the lesson, draw or stamp a clock face on the index cards. Include the numerals to represent the hours, but do not draw hands. Create a list of topics for conversation starters.
2. After gathering both classes in one room, pass out an index card to each student.
3. Demonstrate procedure as follows with a student or the other teacher:
   - Each student finds someone from the other class and forms a pair. The two greet each other with the phrase, "Hi, partner!" or "Hola, compañero/a!"
   - When the teacher calls out a specific hour, each student makes an appointment with his or her partner by writing that person's name on the clock at the given time.
   - When the teacher announces the topic, the partners discuss it for 2 minutes in English and then for 2 minutes in Spanish.
   - When the time is up, each student reports orally in his or her second language any interesting, surprising, or noteworthy information learned about the partner.
   - Partners shake hands or "high five" to say good-bye.
   - All students switch partners and repeat the first five steps until the class period is over.

- Use the appointment cards to form groups during future activities. For example, assign a topic and ask students to discuss it with their "4 o'clock appointment."

4. Begin the activity, use the list of conversation starters, and keep time.

Caveats and Options

1. For the first few pairings, ask students to pair up with people they do not know well.
2. One class period can be devoted to making appointments, saving the topics for a later encounter.
3. The information learned about partners can be used as a writing assignment or reported in interactive journals. The interactive journal (a journal in which the reader responds by writing comments to the writer) can be written by students in one class and shared with the other class. This can be done between individuals or classes, or within a class. The teacher could also be a journal partner.
4. Topics for discussion can be selected by the teachers or developed by the students as a preliminary activity. Suggested topics are favorite food, favorite color, favorite sport, favorite musical group or performer, favorite school subject, memorable trip or experience, embarrassing experience, pets, after-school jobs, and career goals. A special, seasonal topic could be the differences in holiday celebrations. The two classes could celebrate holidays together several times throughout the year.
5. Pair non-Spanish-speaking ESL students with native Spanish speakers of the Spanish class and keep the discussion in English. If there are no native speakers of Spanish in the Spanish class, pair the ESL students with the stronger Spanish students. If there is no shared non-English language among the students, they should conduct the conversation only in English.
6. The ESL class could be grouped with an English language arts class and speak only in English. The English students could then write biographies of the ESL students or report on cultural differences.
7. This activity could pair the ESL class with other foreign language classes. The difficulty is finding an ESL class that is predominantly composed of speakers of other languages commonly found in foreign language classes, such as French, German, Japanese, or Russian.

References and Further Reading

Marzano, R., Pickering, D., Arredondo, D., Blackburn, G., Brandt, R., & Moffett, C. (1992). *Dimensions of learning.* Aurora, CO: McREL Institute.

Omaggio Hadley, A. (1993). *Teaching language in context.* Boston, MA: Heinle & Heinle.

Piper, T. (1993). *Language for all our children.* New York: Macmillan.

Contributors

Diane W. Gómez has taught adult ESL and Spanish in public and parochial schools and residential treatment centers in New York since 1973. Sidonie Schneider has taught ESL and Spanish in Michigan, Maryland, Pennsylvania, and New York since 1973. They both teach at New Rochelle High School in New York, in the United States.

This Is My Freckle!

Levels
Beginning-intermediate

Aims
Learn new content
vocabulary in context
Practice pronunciation,
listening, and speaking
Practice simple sentence
structure using singular
and plural verbs
Learn external parts of
the body

Activity Type
Application or review

Class Time
15-20 minutes

Preparation Time
10 minutes

Resources
None

This simple activity incorporates many skills and is easily adapted to all levels. Although easy at the outset, after several rounds, the challenge heats up. It holds the students' attention as everyone is very keen to see each body part indicated.

Procedure

1. To prepare for the activity, preteach or review vocabulary that may be new for the class (e.g., *knee, ankle, shoulder*). Be sure to include less common vocabulary words such as *dimple, wrinkle,* and *waist.*
2. To begin the activity, have each student (in order of seating arrangement) name and point to an external, visible part of the body. The student must identify it in a complete sentence, for example, "This is my heel." or "These are my eyebrows." Students who do not know the English word may say the word in their native language, and another student or teacher can give the word in English.
3. Continue the activity until each student has had a turn. Then the first student begins again. No body part may be repeated. After several rounds, the activity becomes more challenging.

Caveats and Options

1. For beginners, divide the class into two teams. The teams take turns responding, with each member taking a turn. Ask each team to choose a captain who will write each body part on the board. (The captain does not take a turn while writing.) The activity thus becomes a spelling lesson as well. After each round of the class, a new captain is selected from each team to take a turn writing on the board.

2. This activity can be played with middle- to high-school level students as an "I'm Going to the Doctor" game, similar to "I'm Going on a Picnic." As they take their turns, students repeat the body parts already mentioned (in order) and add a new part. For example, the sixth student might say "I'm going to the doctor and I'm taking my nose, leg, wrist, ankle, chin, and eyebrows!"

3. In general, use only visible, external body parts. This eliminates internal organs, bones, and such, and possible body parts that students may not want to indicate by pointing. You may want to include some parts like *belly button* or *chest* when previewing vocabulary.

4. This game can be supplemented with songs, such as "Head, Shoulders, Knees and Toes," particularly for middle school students.

5. This activity might serve as an introduction to prepare older students to make doctor's appointments or speak to personnel in clinics or emergency rooms.

Contributor

Joyce K. Gianato teaches writing and public speaking at Yonsei University, in Korea. She has an MEd in TESOL from the University of Georgia.

Let Me Tell You About Our Team

Levels
Any

Aims
Develop team identity

Activity Type
Motivation

Class Time
10-15 minutes

Preparation Time
10 minutes

Resources
Copies of the handout
for each student
Two examples of a
completed handout on
the blackboard,
overhead, or poster
paper
Directions for the
activity written on the
blackboard, overhead, or
poster paper

This short activity emphasizes harmony and role-sharing by bringing out characteristics that the group has in common. In this way, the team focuses on identifying with each other, and everyone joins in the fun of the learning together.

Procedure

1. Before class, make a copy of these uncompleted sentences on a handout for each student:

---

1. Our team likes _____ [an activity].

2. We have lots of _____ [object used in activity].

3. We _____ [do this activity] _____ [for example, number of times a day, a week, and so on].

4. Above all, _____ [this activity] makes us _____ [adjective].

5. We are a very _____ [same adjective] team.

Plan to divide your class into teams of four or five. There should be at least one sentence for each member of the team. (In this example, the team has five members.) If your teams have four members, give Student 4 the last two sentences.

2. In class, have your teams sit together in a circle or square. They should already know each other's names. Ask each team to number off from one to four or from one to five.

3. Explain the purpose of the activity. The students should know that this is an enjoyable, brief, warm-up exercise. It is important because it will help them learn how to practice their English better in a team.
4. Tell your teams that you are going to give them four or five sentences. Write these directions on the board or on an overhead transparency:
   - Student 1 is responsible for finding the answer to sentence 1.
   - Student 1 asks for ideas from the other members of the team.
   - Student 1 may not give an answer but can agree or disagree with the suggestions of the others. (No, I don't like to do that. Do you have another idea? Yes, I do that, too. Does everyone like this answer? Good, let's write it down.)
   - Student 2 takes charge of finding the answer for sentence 2.
   - Repeat the process until all the sentences are complete. In this way, no one person dominates, and everyone participates.
5. Give everyone a copy of the sentences. Read the handout together. Show the teams a couple of examples of a completed form on the board.
6. Give your teams 5 minutes to complete the sentences. Each member of the team should have the same answers.
7. Monitor their progress and lend a helping hand to keep things moving.
8. Have the teams report to the class. Each member of the team should read the sentence that he or she was responsible for. (Student 1 should read Sentence 1, and so on.)
9. Praise the team when they have given their report, using descriptive words such as *very clever, smart, original, funny,* and so on. Be sure to convey your surprise and delight over their answers and congratulate them on their effort.

Caveats and Options

1. Do not use more than four or five sentences.
2. If your teams have names, use them in the first sentence instead of "Our team."
3. Create your own sentences for students to complete.
4. Use a spinner to select only one person from each team to present the answers.

5. Include a place on the handout for the students to write the names of everyone on their team.
6. Collect a copy of the handout from each team to post on the classroom bulletin board.

References and Further Reading

Forsyth, D.R. (1990). *Group dynamics*. Pacific Grove, CA: Brooks/Cole.

Kagan, S. (1992). *Cooperative learning*. San Juan Capistrano, CA: Resources for Teachers.

Scholtes, P.R. (1988). *The team handbook: How to use teams effectively*. Madison, WI: Joiner Associates.

Stanford, G. (1977). *Developing effective classroom groups: A practical guide for teachers*. New York: Hart.

Appendix: Sample Team Answers

Example 1: (a straight answer) Our team likes reading. We have lots of books in our homes. We read every night. Above all, reading makes us smart. We are a very smart team.

Example 2: (a playful answer) Our team likes goofing off. We have lots of excuses. We goof off every day. Above all, goofing off makes us happy. We are a very happy team.

Contributor

Wendy Vicens is a lecturer at the American Language and Culture Program at Arizona State University in the United States. She is active in materials development and computer-assisted language learning.

Opinion Maker

Levels
Any; high school

Aims
Get to know one another
Build team spirit
Practice listening and speaking

Activity Type
Motivation

Class Time
20–30 minutes

Preparation Time
15 minutes–1 hour

Resources
Role cards and answer sheet
Timer (or watch or clock with a second hand)
Prize for the winning team (optional)

This activity can be used as an icebreaker or a team-building activity when cooperative learning groups are being assigned. The purpose of the game is to reach group consensus within the allotted time (4 minutes). The groups compete with one another to win.

Procedure

1. Make the role cards for each team:

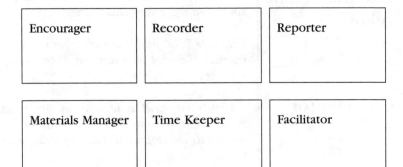

Encourager	Recorder	Reporter
Materials Manager	Time Keeper	Facilitator

2. Prepare the answer sheet. See sample in Appendix.
3. Organize the cooperative learning groups. There should be no more than six students per group.
4. Ask the students to join their assigned groups.
5. Hand out the role cards. Give the students 1 minute to choose their roles.
6. Explain that this is an activity designed to improve listening and speaking skills as well as team building and consensus building. Tell

the students that they will have 4 minutes to complete the activity; the group with the most points wins.

7. Ask the materials manager to get the answer sheet for his or her group from you. Set the timer for 4 minutes. Tell the students they have only 4 minutes to come up with a food that all of them like, and one they all dislike; a TV program that all of them like and one they all dislike; a politician they all like and one they all dislike; and a song they all like and one they all dislike. If they sing the song they like (or dislike), they will get 5 points for that category. If they sing *and* put the song to motion, they will get 10 points. Each other category is worth 1 point.

8. Remind students that the goal is to reach consensus quickly, not to change people's minds about their likes or dislikes.

9. While the students are trying to reach consensus, circulate to be sure they are on the right track. When the 4 minutes are up, pick up the answer sheet from each team and quickly score it. Ask the students to sing or dance for extra credit.

10. Debrief according to the purpose for the activity. Ask students their opinion of the activity.

Caveats and Options

1. Once the answer sheets are collected, they could be handed to different groups to score and read aloud.

2. If the groups are of mixed ability levels, you may want to assign the roles yourself.

3. An optional scoring method is to offer points only to groups that have unique responses. So, if two groups chose pizza as a food they like, neither group would get a point for that response. If this scoring method is used, the students should be informed in advance.

Acknowledgments

I experienced this type of activity in a workshop entitled, "How to Develop Masterful Presentations," sponsored by the Association for Supervision and Curriculum Development and presented by Robert Garmston and Suzanne Bailey in Washington, DC, June 1994.

Appendix: Sample Answer Sheet for Opinion Maker

	Like	Dislike
Food		
TV Program		
Politician		
Song		

Contributor

Emily Lynch Gómez has been in the ESL/EFL profession for more than 10 years. She currently works at the Center for Applied Linguistics, in Washington, DC, on the TESOL ESL Standards and Assessment Project.

Celebrate Me: Writing an Autobiography

Levels
Any; middle school

Aims
Learn the steps of the
writing process
Practice creative expres-
sion and original thought
Use a dictionary
Work cooperatively
Give oral presentations
to the class
Increase self-esteem

Activity Type
Presentation of
information
Practice, application, motivation, or assessment

Class Time
Approximately ten
45-minute class periods

Preparation Time
15 minutes

Resources
Construction paper
Plain white paper
Yarn
Hole punch
Scissors
Dictionaries

This class project can be used as a school-year opener to teach students the basic steps of the writing process while simultaneously assessing their linguistic abilities and personal interests. Because students work cooperatively to create their own autobiographies, it is a good way to break the ice during the first days of class.

Procedure

1. Introduce the project. Explain to the students that they will be writing their own "Celebrate Me" books. Discuss the concept of celebration and what students think it means to "celebrate me." Also discuss the meaning of autobiography and ask students what kinds of information they think an autobiography should include. Make a list of their ideas.

2. Give students a piece of construction paper to make a book cover. Have them fold it in half and decorate the cover at home using drawings, photographs, magazine cutouts, or anything that reflects their interests or personality.

3. The next day, give students three sheets of plain white paper. Have them fold the paper in half to fit inside the book cover. Demonstrate how to use a hole-punch to punch through the book cover and inside pages. Run a piece of yarn through the holes to tie the book together. Have the students construct their books.

4. Explain to the students that their books will have 12 pages; each page for a different topic. They will use the steps of the writing process to write their pages. You can have students invent their own topics, use the list made in Step 1, or if the students are reluctant, suggest some of these: Personal Information, My Family, My Best Friend(s), My Free Time, Something That Makes Me Proud, If I Had Three Wishes, A Skill

I Would Like to Learn, Countries I Have Lived In or Visited, Languages I Speak, and so on. Then, discuss the steps of the writing process. Students will need a partner for Steps 3 and 5. You can have them choose their own partners or pair them up as you see fit. Steps 1–5 should be done in class. Step 6 can be done at home, saving class time and allowing students time to be creative with the final copy.

Step 1: Prewriting—Brainstorm ideas for each topic, writing them down in notes or lists. No need to use complete sentences; just get ideas on paper.

Step 2: Drafting—Using your notes from Step 1, write your first draft on notebook paper. Do not worry about spelling or grammar; just write your notes and ideas in sentence form.

Step 3: Conferencing—Share your first draft with your partner. Your partner will tell you what he or she likes about it as well as how it can be better.

Step 4: Revising—Using what you learned from Step 3, make changes to your draft.

Step 5: Proofreading—Look for mistakes in spelling, capitalization, punctuation, and grammar. Ask your partner or teacher to help you, and use a dictionary.

Step 6: Publishing—Copy the final draft neatly into your "Celebrate Me" book. Include a title and page number for each page. Add photos, magazine pictures, or drawings to make your book more exciting.

5. Have students present their completed books orally to the class. Have them read favorite parts, tell what they liked and disliked about the project, tell what they would like to have done differently, and so on. You may also want to make a bulletin board display for everyone to enjoy.

Caveats and Options

1. Allow beginners to write first in their native language and then translate into English to make the task seem less forbidding. Adjust your expectations according to students' linguistic abilities.
2. The length of time it takes to complete the project can easily be adjusted by increasing or decreasing the number of pages in the book. You can use all or some of the pages, depending on the needs and nature of your class.
3. If assessment of the project is a concern, try giving a holistic grade for writing (process and product), creativity (effort over artistic ability), and neatness (a presentable final product), and average the three grades for an overall grade.
4. Have students vote by secret ballot on the best book (or top three) and give special recognition to the "winners."
5. You may want to make a display of the books in the school library for others to enjoy.

References and Further Reading

Lipson, G.B. (1989). *Fast ideas for busy teachers.* Carthage, IL: Good Apple.

Contributor

Denise Albrecht Sullivan received her MA in TEFL from the American University in Cairo. She currently teaches secondary ESL at the American International School in Egypt.

◆ Getting to Know Your School Fun Hunt

Levels
Any

Aims
Read and follow
directions
Sequence information
Practice real-life
situations
Make decisions
Work cooperatively

Activity Type
Motivation or
application

Class Time
30–45 minutes

Preparation Time
1–2 hours

Resources
Clock or watch with a
second hand
5-in. x 8-in. index cards
List of team members
(made by teacher)
Pens or pencils (one for
each team)

For this activity, a Spanish class works with a predominantly Spanish-speaking ESL class. The task provides both groups the opportunity for a multicultural exchange and stimulates conversation in a real-life situation.

Procedure

1. Join the Spanish and ESL classes and divide students into teams of three or four members before the lesson begins. Where possible, each team should have at least one student from the Spanish class and one from the ESL class.

2. Prepare progressive and sequential written directions to several locations in the school building and ask the team to record something specific at each location. The first set of directions should start at the classroom. When the students reach the first site, they record the information needed. The next set of directions begins at that first site, and so on. For example:

   ● Turn left as you leave our classroom door. Go straight. At the first corridor, turn right. Go to the third door on the right. Write the number of the door you are facing. _____.

   ● Continue down the hall. Walk about 50 feet. Turn left. Continue straight. Look on the wall. Write the name of two women on the Board of Education. _____ and _____ . (There is a plaque on the wall with a list of Board members.)

3. Prepare enough cards for each team, each with between five and eight sets of directions. Each team should receive a different set of directions.

4. Tell the students that the first team to return with their cards completed accurately in the least amount of time wins.

5. Give the first group the "go" signal and record their starting time on the team list. Stagger the starting times at about 1-minute intervals.

6. As groups return, record the return time, and check the card for accuracy.

7. Determine the winning team and announce the winners.

Caveats and Options

1. Ask supervisors/school officials for permission to do the hunt.

2. Notify security officers of the time and date of the hunt.

3. Discuss proper behavior expected in the halls.

4. Keep the list of directions equal in number, difficulty, and distance for each team.

5. The directions can be developed by the teacher or by the students as a pre-activity. This is an opportunity to review key directional words and school-related vocabulary, if needed.

6. Prizes can be awarded. Rewards or privileges, such as a free pass to skip homework for one night can be given instead of real objects.

7. Graphs, such as bar graphs, can be made to chart the results of each team in the hunt.

8. The preparation of the activity may be time-consuming the first year it is used, but it can be repeated year after year.

9. Measurements in feet and yards can be made before the hunt so that they can be included in the directions.

10. Students can draw maps of their journey through the school.

11. Students from other classes (e.g., English, Spanish, social studies) can improve their clarity of writing by developing directions for each ESL team.

12. This activity could be done with just the ESL class, but the mixing of two classes benefits each class socioculturally.

References and Further Reading

Marzano, R., Pickering, D., Arredondo, D., Blackburn, G., Brandt, R., & Moffett, C. (1992). *Dimensions of learning.* Aurora, CO: McREL Institute.

Omaggio Hadley, A. (1993). *Teaching language in context.* Boston: Heinle & Heinle.

Contributor

Diane W. Gómez has taught adult ESL and Spanish in public and parochial schools and residential treatment centers in New York since 1973. She currently teaches high school Spanish and is working on her doctorate.

What's Happening?

Levels
Beginning; high school

Aims
Review vocabulary for
school places and
subjects
Practice present
continuous tense
Write a composition
about activities in the
school
Practice listening and
speaking

Activity Type
Application or review

Class Time
2 hours

Preparation Time
1 hour

Resources
School vocabulary
picture handout
Notebooks and pencils
for the reporters

This activity can reinforce school orientation and curriculum information as well as help students practice specific language structures. Acting as reporters, students tour selected places in the school, observe what is going on in each place, and use their notes to write a composition describing the daily routine at school.

Procedure

1. If you have access to the book *Practical Vocabulary Builder* (Liebowicz, 1988), use the handout called "School" to review places in the school such as library, cafeteria, gym, water fountain, lockers, and computer lab. Otherwise, you can draw appropriate illustrations. Supplement, if necessary, by eliciting other places from the students or adding others yourself, and write the place names on the board.

2. Review present continuous tense by questioning what students in the class are doing. For example, "What's Juan doing now?" "He's writing." You may want to practice both singular and plural third person forms. Have students write models in their notebooks.

3. Explain to students that they are reporters who are going to write about what is happening at school today. As they visit each place, they should take notes about where they are and what people are doing. Put an example on the board, such as *cafeteria—eating*. Explain they will write a composition later and their notes can be used to create sentences, such as "In the cafeteria, students are eating."

4. Guide the students on a tour of select places in the school. As you pause in or outside each location, pose questions such as: "What are they doing?" "What is that boy doing?" "What do you see?" Repeat answers that students give to confirm the activity and reinforce language structures and pronunciation, such as "Yes. A boy is typing

in the computer lab." "Girls are playing volleyball in the gym." Ask students to take notes and, as needed, encourage students to ask you about spelling as you describe activities.

5. When you return to the classroom, provide a model composition for the students. Review essential components of the composition, such as introductory topic sentence, details, indentation, and capitalization.

6. Allow the students time to write a draft of their composition, titled: "What's Happening at _____ (your school name)." Circulate to provide individual assistance. Students need not include all the information from their notes, and individual compositions should vary.

7. Have students share their drafts with partners or in small groups so they can see which places and activities were described.

8. If possible, have the reporters enter their final copy on the computer, using a word-processing program.

Caveats and Options

1. You may need to secure permission before you visit certain places or classes in the school.

2. Caution students to be quiet so they do not disturb the activities in progress.

3. Try this activity at different times of day to focus on different places and activities.

4. You can adapt this activity to include other personnel and their activities, such as, "The secretary is talking on the phone." "The custodian is cleaning the floor."

5. If you do not have access to the vocabulary builder ditto or blackline master, you may want to use pictures of school places found in the school yearbook, guidance brochures, or other school publications.

6. You may ask students to illustrate their compositions and then display their work in the classroom or on a bulletin board in the hall.

References and Further Reading

Liebowicz, D.G. (1988). *Practical vocabulary builder.* Lincolnwood, IL: National Textbook Company.

Contributor

Carolyn Bohlman's 20 years in ESL include teaching adults and secondary students as well as working as a consultant and teacher trainer.

The Library: Check It Out!

Levels
High beginning

Aims
Review vocabulary
Become familiar with
the school library and
its resources

Activity Type
Assessment or review

Class Time
2 hours

Preparation Time
30 minutes

Resources
Illustrations, visuals
about the library
Library-related objects
(e.g., books, magazines,
encyclopedia)
School librarian
Word bank
Scavenger hunt handout

This activity is a hands-on assessment of student understanding of the school library and its human and material resources. Even less proficient students can become comfortable with this resource through level-appropriate activities.

Procedure

1. With the school librarian, plan a modified tour that highlights library resources.
2. Begin an orientation to the library in the classroom through the use of illustrations, visuals, and realia. Use the map in Appendix A or develop one of your own library.
3. Create a word bank of essential vocabulary words that will initially be taught in the classroom, associated with realia when possible, and reinforced by the librarian once the students go to the library.
4. Have the librarian give the students a tour of the library.
5. Distribute a scavenger hunt handout to students (see sample in Appendix B) to provide practice in actually using the library.
6. As students complete each task, ask them to have you or the librarian initial the list to verify completion.

Caveats and Options

1. Before you give students the hands-on activity, you may need to review vocabulary, for example with a matching or fill-in-the-blank exercise to define terms.
2. Alert your librarian to the English-proficiency level of your students so that explanations during the library tour will be appropriate.
3. Allow enough time for students to complete the scavenger hunt tasks during one class period so they do not lose momentum.

4. Tell students that they do not have to start with Number 1. They may start with any task as long as they complete all of them.

5. For students at this level, you may want to have your librarian demonstrate how to find a book through the computerized catalog. It may be preferable to reserve further instruction and student practice of this activity for more proficient students.

References and Further Reading

Maggs, M. (1983). *English across the curriculum. Book 2.* Lincolnwood, IL: National Textbook Co.

Schinke-Llano, L. (1985). *Advanced vocabulary games for English language users.* Lincolnwood, IL: National Textbook Co.

Appendix A: Sample Map of Library

Your Library

Credit: Designed by Donna Hahn, Librarian at Maine Township High School East, Parkridge, IL. Used with permission.

Word Bank

bilingual dictionary	biography	book
book drop	book mark	circulation desk
check out	computer	copy machine
computerized card catalog	due date	encyclopedia
fiction	library	librarian
magazine	newspaper	paperback
print	renew	screen
	shelf	

Appendix B: Check It Out! A Library Scavenger Hunt

_____ 1. Find today's newspaper. Who is in the news?

_____ 2. Find a bilingual dictionary with your first language and English. Show it to your teacher.

_____ 3. Find the copy machine. How much does one copy cost?

_____ 4. Check the list of magazines. Write the names of two magazines that you looked at.

_____ 5. Find a book that you like. Check it out. What is the due date?_____

Write the title here:_____

Show the book to your teacher.

_____ 6. When is the library open?_____

_____ 7. Ask the librarian one question about the library. Write your question here:

_____

Contributor

Carolyn Bohlman has taught adults and secondary ESL students. She has also worked as a statewide ESL consultant to adult education programs in Illinois, in the United States.

Part II: Integrated Language Development Activities

Editor's Note

This section offers a diverse mix of language development activities categorized into the following sets: vocabulary, listening and speaking, reading, and writing. Although this classification system is useful, it hides the real story behind most of the activities, for many of the contributions encourage students to develop more than one language skill. In those cases, students may apply the indicated skill to other language development processes.

The vocabulary activities include three enjoyable crossword variations and several contributions that help students recognize the relationships among words. Other activities help students understand vocabulary in context.

The listening and speaking set begins with listening comprehension activities that integrate music and activities that focus on following and giving directions and on pronunciation. Later activities help students practice conversational speech and academic skills such as discussing observations and generating oral summaries. This set finishes with activities designed to help students give oral presentations.

A common thread running through the set of reading activities is the notion that students should read for a purpose. The activities include both pleasure reading and academic reading, encouraging students to respond personally to the text, summarize, take notes, make judgments, and share with other students information learned through reading.

The writing set opens with an awareness activity to help students recognize the importance of detail in writing and then a sentence-building activity. The activities that follow move students through the writing process using a variety of strategies. Students are asked to write about themselves and their experiences in paragraphs and through original stories, individually and in groups. They are also asked to create stories in response to visual clues and story starters.

◆ Developing Language Through Vocabulary Building
Creative Crosswords

Levels
Any

Aims
Increase speaking
fluency
Practice listening
Build general and
specific vocabulary

Activity Type
Motivation, practice, or
review

Class Time
15 minutes

Preparation Time
15 minutes

Resources
Crossword puzzle with
words at students' skill
level

This exercise turns crossword puzzles into a communicative activity by having students create their own clues for the answers in an information-gap format.

Procedure

1. Take two copies of the same crossword puzzle. Cut off the clues and throw them away. Write all the horizontal answers on one copy, and all the vertical answers on the other copy. Label one sheet Student A and the other Student B. Make copies of the sheets so that half the class will be As, and the other half will be Bs.
2. Pair students and hand out puzzles so that partners have contrasting puzzles.
3. Student A looks at the missing words and asks Student B what one of them is, for example, "What is number 3 across?" Student B finds the word (written on his or her puzzle) and answers with a clue. For example, if the word were *subway,* Student B might say, "This is a train that runs under the ground." Student A guesses at the word. If the guess is incorrect, Student B gives more clues, as needed. When the correct word is guessed, Student A writes it into the puzzle.
4. Next, Student B asks Student A. Play continues until the two finish.

Caveats and Options

1. The partners can be switched at any time during the activity. As long as As are with Bs, the hint-giving can continue without any overlap.

2. Students may need to practice thinking up clues to the words in the puzzle. This could be done in advance with sample words.

3. For clues, students may use definitions, antonyms, synonyms, sounds, gestures, or doodles, if desired. Dictionaries or other students with the same designation (A or B) could be consulted for unknown words.

4. Students can develop their own crosswords according to course-specific criteria using puzzle software. Crossword puzzle software exists which makes it very easy to adapt this activity to specific vocabulary words. The software can be found on an Internet search and can either be purchased or downloaded without charge.

References and Further Reading

Insight Software Solutions. (1997). *Crossword construction kit*. Bountiful, UT: Author. (Available by mail from Insight Software Solutions, Inc., PO Box 354, Bountiful, UT 84011 USA. Tel. 801-299-1781. URL www.crosswordkit .com)

Contributor

Elizabeth Bigler has taught EFL in Japan and ESL in the United States in academic, adult, and refugee programs. Her MS in applied linguistics/ ESL is from Georgia State University.

Crossquiz Puzzle

Levels
Intermediate +

Aims
Develop vocabulary
skills
Review content and
language structures
Practice reading and
writing

Activity Type
Assessment or review

Class Time
2 hours

Preparation Time
1–2 hours

Resources
Handout with grid
Word cards with
vocabulary and
structures covered in
the unit of study

This activity can be used as a review or assessment of student knowledge of the content and structures studied over a period of time or in a unit. At the same time, the students have fun creating and solving crossword puzzles.

Procedure

1. Together with the students, prepare a list of concepts, vocabulary, and structures to be assessed or reviewed.
2. Prepare word cards with definition words or structures and any other relevant content. There is no limit to the number of letters in the words; phrases can also be included. For example, if the class has been studying a unit on plants, some of the terms for the word cards could be: *roots, photosynthesis, leaves, seeds, chlorophyll, grow, plant, water,* and so on. Make enough cards to give each student at least two. Word cards may be repeated.
3. Seat students in small groups of three to five.
4. Ask each group to select at random a number of cards (not less than two per student).
5. Give each group the handout with the grid (see Appendix).
6. Ask each group to prepare a crossword puzzle using the word cards. For each word card, they must write the explanation or definition for the down or across clues. The clues for structures may be sentences where the space for the structure is a blank space (e.g., *The plant has _____ one centimeter this week.*).
7. Once finished, groups are asked to exchange crosswords and solve them.
8. A third group may be asked to edit a puzzle, giving each group the opportunity to create a puzzle, solve another one, and edit a third one.

36

9. After editing, the third group will give the crossword back to the authoring group to create the final version.
10. Discuss all the crosswords with the whole class.
11. Check each crossword for content, spelling of words, grammar, and mechanics (e.g., capitalization, punctuation).

Caveats and Options

1. This activity may be used as a source for content to be included in tests given at the end of a unit of study or a marking period.
2. If the activity is planned as a review, allow the students to use their notes and books. However, if it is planned as a group assessment, make sure students are familiar with crosswords in general and ask them to write the crossword clues using the knowledge they have previously acquired. They can consult only with the other members of their group. In this way, each crossword will be a separate assessment measure for each group.
3. To evaluate if group work is helping individuals in the learning process, give a short quiz to every member of each group about the terms contained in the crossword they created and in the one they solved.
4. This activity is especially good for content-based ESL science and social studies classes where students must learn many concepts in each unit.
5. This activity may be done without giving the students any word cards. Each group has the option to use all the concepts they remember from a given topic or lesson. In this way, you can notice which concepts are ignored or misinterpreted by the class.
6. The crossword made by the students may be used as part of their group portfolios, as a sample of their writing abilities and knowledge of subject matter.

References and Further Reading

Genesee, F., & Upshur, J. (1996). *Classroom based evaluation in second language education.* New York: Cambridge University Press.

McCloskey, M.L. (1990). *Integrated language teaching strategies.* Atlanta, GA: Educo Press.

Murphey, T. (1995). Tests: Learning through negotiated interaction. *TESOL Journal, 4*(2), 12–16.

Appendix: Sample Puzzle

Create Your Own Crossquiz Puzzle

Team members: _____

Title: _____

Clues

ACROSS: DOWN:

Solved by: _____

Contributor

Dafne Gonzalez has coordinated an EFL program (elementary and high school levels) for 10 years in a private school in Venezuela.

Using Student-Generated Crossword Puzzles to Build Vocabulary

Levels
Advanced; high school

Aims
Learn how to spell and define vocabulary words

Activity Type
Practice or review

Class Time
50 minutes

Preparation Time
20 minutes

Resources
Graph paper
Dictionary

This activity provides an enjoyable yet challenging tool for students to review the spelling and meaning of vocabulary words.

Procedure

1. Give each student at least three sheets of graph paper.

2. Write a list of 10–15 thematically linked vocabulary words on the board. Linking vocabulary through a theme will help students learn the words and relate them to a subject.

3. On one sheet of graph paper, have students write the vocabulary words following a crossword puzzle format (see Appendix as a guide for Steps 3–8). Students should begin with a long word, find another word with a common letter, and connect them through that letter. They should alternate placing words down and across, connecting them at their common letter. Make sure that students connect each word correctly and do not juxtapose words. They should not place words in a diagonal line. This sheet will serve as the answer key.

4. Give students a second sheet of graph paper to place on top of the first sheet. Tell students to draw lines around each box containing a letter. This sheet will be the skeleton crossword puzzle.

5. Show students how to number the rows and columns on the skeleton crossword puzzle. The box with the first letter of the word closest to the uppermost left corner of the puzzle will be numbered 1 regardless of whether it is a row or column. Next move toward the right, along the same line. If there is a box that begins another word (column or row), place No. 2 in that box. Continue numbering along

the same row until there are no more boxes which begin a new word. Move to the next row down, and, again moving from left to right, number all boxes which house the beginning of a word. Continue in this fashion until all boxes containing the initial letter of a puzzle word have a number. Some rows or columns may share a number. Do not put two different numbers in the same box. Do not use the same number twice. Copy this numbering system onto the answer key.

6. Distribute a third sheet of paper and tell students to make two sections, one labeled *Across* and the second labeled *Down.*

7. On the section labeled *Across,* ask students to write down all of the numbers that represent words in rows found on their puzzles. After each number they should write a definition of the word represented by that number. Students should follow similar directions for the *Down* section, writing the numbers that represent words in columns and the definitions.

8. Ask students to check their crossword puzzles carefully for correct spelling and definitions, and to ensure that the definitions and numbers correspond to the words in the puzzle.

9. Ask students to exchange their crossword puzzles and to complete the new one they receive. This will help them review the vocabulary words—their spelling and meaning—one more time.

Caveats and Options

1. Students should know how to complete a crossword puzzle before they engage in this activity.

2. Students can work in groups to design their crossword puzzles.

3. Students should use a pencil as some words may need to be changed.

4. If your class is not working with thematic units, gather vocabulary words for the crosswords from a specific reading (e.g., a story, a chapter in a class textbook,) a video shown in class, or any other curricular material used in the class.

Appendix: Sample Crossword Puzzle and Steps

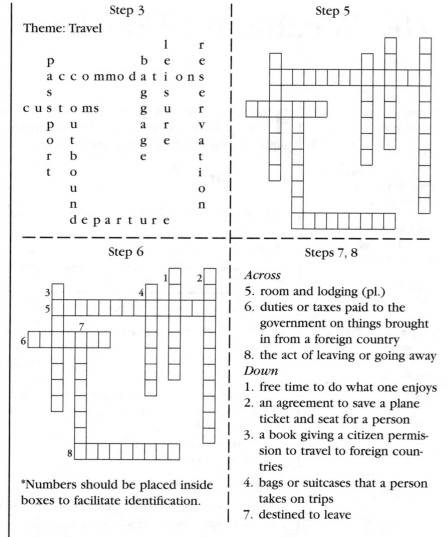

Step 3

Theme: Travel

Step 5

Step 6

*Numbers should be placed inside boxes to facilitate identification.

Steps 7, 8

Across
5. room and lodging (pl.)
6. duties or taxes paid to the government on things brought in from a foreign country
8. the act of leaving or going away

Down
1. free time to do what one enjoys
2. an agreement to save a plane ticket and seat for a person
3. a book giving a citizen permission to travel to foreign countries
4. bags or suitcases that a person takes on trips
7. destined to leave

Contributor

Maya Alvarez taught ESL in high school in California and is currently working on her PhD at the University of Southern California, in the United States.

The Vocabulary Continuum

Levels
Intermediate

Aims
Develop vocabulary
Practice writing and
speaking

Activity Type
Presentation of
information

Class Time
10–15 minutes

Preparation Time
20 minutes

Resources
Thesaurus
Overhead projector or
chalkboard

This activity is used to help students refine their vocabularies and better understand the shadings of difference between words. The activity supports more effective writing and speaking.

Procedure

1. Decide on a number of vocabulary words that represent a range along a continuum, such as

   <———————————————————————————————>
   scalding   hot   warm   tepid   cool   chilling   frigid

   <———————————————————————————————>
   frantic   upset   anxious   calm   subdued   comatose

2. Present the words in random order on index cards. The index cards can be moved easily in the process of determining the continuum. The words can also be presented on a list on the overhead projector or the board and then written on a blank continuum line on a piece of paper. This technique is not as flexible, but it does have the student practice writing the words and it can then be kept for future reference in a writing notebook.

3. Have students work individually or in pairs to place the words along the blank continuum.

   <———————————————————————————————>

4. Have students compare their continuum with those generated by other students or pairs and arrive at a final consensus.

Caveats and Options

1. Students may be given only the two words at each end of the continuum and be asked to generate words in the middle. As another variation, they may be given only a word in the middle and asked to think of words that move outward in both directions.
2. Students may be asked to generate sentences using each word.
3. Students may be asked to role-play each word.
4. Offer students clozelike sentences and ask them to choose which word from the continuum is most appropriate and why.
5. Students should be encouraged to look for new words that might fit a continuum in their reading assignments and activities. Words to be used on the continuum may be taken from the students' oral and written language.
6. To modify this activity for beginning students, select fewer, easier words, such as *run, walk, jog*.
7. Introduce beginning students to words along the continuum in an experiential way, through demonstrations or illustrations.

References and Further Reading

Bromley, K., Irwin-DeVitis, L., & Modlo, M. (1995). *Graphic organizers: Visual strategy for active learning*. New York: Scholastic Professional Books.

Contributor

Linda Irwin-DeVitis taught high school ESL in Louisiana and is on the reading and language arts faculty at Binghamton University in the state of New York, in the United States.

Who Did This?

Levels
Intermediate; high school

Aims
Discover word meaning from context

Activity Type
Motivation

Class Time
50 minutes

Preparation Time
50 minutes

Resources
Four or five sentences with vocabulary unknown to the students

Reading may be slow and frustrating for students because they insist on looking up all the words they do not know. This group activity is an enjoyable demonstration of the value of guessing from context, and encourages students to rely less heavily on their dictionaries.

Procedure

1. Choose a paragraph with challenging, unfamiliar vocabulary items in at least four sentences and prepare a simple matching quiz with these words. Identify the four sentences as A, B, C, D. Type them on separate sheets of paper along with a list of questions that helps clarify the meaning of each vocabulary word. (See Appendix A.)
2. Put the sentences up on the classroom walls, spacing them out so that four people can study each without crowding. Arrange the students in home groups of four students and assign each student a letter: A, B, C, D. Hand out the quiz, one copy for each group, so the students will recognize the challenge. Tell them the quiz will be used later.
3. Use questions to demonstrate how to arrive at a general meaning. A nonsense sentence works well. (*The kuge benily prapped the hobentates with a tossip elna.*) Who did this? What did he do? When? How? To what or whom? With what? What kind? A corresponding meaningful sentence is also useful. (The cook quickly chopped the vegetables with a sharp houchow.)
4. Instruct the members to leave their home groups to study their respective sentences on the wall. They may confer with the members from other groups who share their letter designation until they think they understand the meaning of their words. When they return to their seats, allow equal time for members A–D to teach their items and fill in the answers on the quiz. Collect the quiz from each of the

groups and discuss the answers as a whole class. This is a good time to practice other unfamiliar words in the sentences.

Caveats and Options

1. Before class discussion of the quiz, distribute copies of the whole paragraph to each group for more complete understanding. (See Appendix B.)
2. For advanced students, more than one unfamiliar word from each sentence can be selected for the quiz.
3. Choose advertisements from popular magazines that include pictures and creative or playful use of language instead of textbook sentences.
4. Be careful students do not use a dictionary.

Appendix A: Sample Vocabulary Quiz

Directions: Beside the numbers of each word in the left column, write the letter of the word or phrase on the right that has almost the same meaning.

_____ 1. computations	A. many
_____ 2. evolve	B. change
_____ 3. merely	C. mathematics
_____ 4. manifold	D. only

Sentences for Group Practice

A. Computers have been important in business for the past four decades, *evolving* through several generations, but their history begins much earlier.

Sample clarification questions: What did computers do through several generations? Did they stay the same? Can you think of a word to use in the place of *evolving*?

B. Although computers today do much more than *merely* solve problems with numbers, they began with instruments such as the abacus, a special device made of beads strung on wires and used for counting.

Questions: What do computers do now? What did they do at the beginning? Do you think the word *merely* is probably closer in meaning to (a) more or (b) less?

C. Other mathematical devices invented before the computer were the slide rule and mechanical calculators, which could do *computations* much more quickly and accurately than a human being could.

Questions: Which of the following is probably closest in meaning to *computation*? (a) slide rule (b) accurately (c) math

D. Huge books were used to hold tables and formulas that helped people perform *manifold* long and difficult mathematical procedures.

Questions: What did the tables and formulas help people do? What did the people perform? What kind? How many?

Appendix B: Sample Paragraph

Computers have been commercially important for the past four decades, evolving through several generations, but their history begins much earlier. Although computers today do much more than merely solve problems with numbers, if we look for the beginning of the history of computers, we find it in ancient mathematical instruments such as the abacus, a special device made of beads strung on wires and used for calculating mathematical sums. Other ancestors were the slide rule and mechanical calculators, which could make computations much more quickly and accurately than a human being could. Huge books were used to hold tables and formulas that helped people perform manifold long and difficult mathematical procedures. These are the tasks that computers today do so quickly and so well.

Contributor

Janet Caglan is a lecturer in the College of Extended Education at Arizona State University in the United States.

Creating Conversational Contexts for Reading Vocabulary

Levels
High beginning +

Aims
Practice reading
vocabulary in a
conversational format
Develop meaningful con-
trol of vocabulary words
Practice language
functions and grammar
informally
Develop imagination,
general knowledge, crit-
ical thinking skills, and
intercultural awareness

Activity Type
Application or assessment

Class Time
20–30 minutes for 10
vocabulary words

Preparation Time
15–30 minutes,
depending on the
teacher's imagination

Resources
Vocabulary words from
lessons, readings, and
units
List of conversational
contexts

Although ESL students can often memorize words and definitions, they may have great difficulty placing vocabulary words in context and using words in original sentences—skills that promote ownership of words. This activity provides meaningful practice by creating conversational contexts, that is, partial contexts with new vocabulary that students complete with an item of information, phrase, or clause.

Procedure

1. Create the conversational contexts for new vocabulary words. This is a three-step process using notions, functions/content, and grammar in a schema drawn from the author's experience using the *World of Vocabulary* series. (See Appendix A.) Use this schema to devise contexts that include a range of conversational forms and structures:

   ● First, select a notion. Six categories of notions will embrace most new vocabulary items: examples; habits; evaluations; values and opinions; speculations and wishes; and explanations.

   ● Second, choose the function or content within the category.

   ● Third, add an appropriate grammar focus.

   For example, the word *passengers* appears in a reading about Venice, Italy. The context is the notion category of "examples," with cultural information as the content and present tense as the grammar focus. Students would complete a sentence context like: "Buses in my country hold _____ *passengers*." by filling in the blank with a number (e.g., 35) or other words (e.g., cargo and), and then discussing the answers. For the word *regulated* in the same reading, the notion category of "Values and Opinions" could be chosen with cultural information and modals of obligation (e.g., should/shouldn't) for the class to discuss school dress codes in the context. "The clothes students wear to school should/shouldn't be *regulated* because _____." Students complete the sentence and discuss their opinions. (Sample conversational contexts appear in Appendix B.)

2. Complete your usual presentation of new vocabulary (e.g., new words in the context of a reading) and initial activities to construct meaning via definitions, examples, and illustrations.

3. Distribute the conversational contexts to your students. Allow sufficient time for them to think about answers or assign them for homework so students will have answers to share for conversation during the next class.

4. For the conversation period, work with the entire class or in small groups. In the full class, have students state their answers. When working in small groups, have group members choose a representative answer to be shared with the entire class, either as a group effort or by selecting the best of the homework answers discussed in the group. In both cases, once answers have been shared, encourage others to build on their classmates' answers to generate a discussion, by asking additional questions, providing additional information or examples, or offering comments.

5. Focus on multicultural responses that arise. For example, in discussing if school clothes should be *regulated*, interesting commentary may arise about uniforms and other aspects of education in other countries' schools. In some cases, the extended conversation can help promote intercultural understanding.

6. Use the teachable moment to probe, illustrate, clarify, seek more information, or broaden the context. For example, the context of Sentence 4 for *canals* (in Appendix B) usually elicits the Panama Canal, but discussion can lead to the Suez Canal, the Erie Canal, or the canal networks of ancient China.

7. Incorporate these contexts as a feature of your vocabulary testing as an alternate way of assessing student understanding.

Caveats and Options

1. Give several sample answers where necessary, especially when introducing the activity for the first time or for handling the "I don't know" answers. Students can choose from these examples to complete the contexts. A sample schema of notions, function/content, and grammar is given in Appendix A.

2. Anticipate materials for illustration to the extent possible. For example, in the *canals* context mentioned above, maps are helpful to pinpoint the locations of the canals discussed. Pictures and other realia also prove useful.

3. Involve all students in conversation, not just the more outgoing. To work around cultural or individual reluctance to talk about oneself, substitute *people from my country* for *I*.

4. Provide prompts as needed to help delineate responses. Frame these as *wh*-questions under the answer lines or at the end of the context sentences. (See bracketed items in Appendix B.)

5. Include your own answers in the discussion to enliven the conversation and hold student interest.

References and Further Reading

Rauch, S.J., & Clements, Z.J. (1991). *World of vocabulary, aqua level.* New York: Globe.

Appendix A: Sample Schema of Notions, Functions, and Grammar

Notion	Function/Content	Grammar Point
A. Examples	Actions Characteristics, qualities Time, cultural and personal information	Present
B. Habits	Personal Family Cultural	Frequency adverbs

C. Evaluations	Comparing and
	  contrasting
		Comparatives and
		  superlatives

D. Values and opinions	Likes or dislikes Obligations	Present tense Negatives Modals
E. Speculations and wishes	*I hope, I'd like to*	Conditionals
F. Explanations	Reasons Cause and effect	Subordinates Conjunctions

Appendix B: Sample Conversational Contexts

The following conversational contexts illustrate schema categories from a text in *World of Vocabulary, Aqua Level,* "A City Without Roads." The reading describes Venice as a city of canals and emphasizes the transportation system of gondolas and water-buses. The new vocabulary presented in the reading is highlighted in each context. The letter of the context category from the schema is included. (Some examples fit multiple categories. See Caveat 1.) Sample responses from a student appear in the answer spaces.

1. Buses in my country hold about_40_ *passengers*. (A)

2. The oldest building where I come from was *erected* about 2,000 years ago. (A) [How many?]

3. I usually *prefer* to drink orange juice at lunch and dinner. (B) [What?]

4. One of the world's most famous *canals* is <u>the Panama Canal</u>. (C)

5. You should try to get *tickets* to a concert by <u>Aerosmith</u>. (D) [Which group?]

6. The clothes students wear to schools should be *regulated* because <u>you can wear a uniform and not spend a lot of money buying many clothes</u>. (D/F)

7. I would like to take a vacation in the <u>Hawaiian</u> *Islands* where I would <u>swim and see a lot of girls</u>. (E) [Where? and Why?]

8. Riding in a *gondola* would be romantic because <u>they are slow, and if you are with a date, that'll be even more romantic</u>. (E/F).

Contributor

Joseph E. Leaf has taught ESL at the secondary level for 20 years in the Norristown Area School District in Pennsylvania, in the United States.

◆ Developing Language Through Listening and Speaking

Get Cloze With Music

Levels
Intermediate +

Aims
Improve listening,
pronunciation, writing,
and reading skills
Practice negotiating

Activity Type
Motivation or
enrichment

Class Time
45 minutes

Preparation Time
30-60 minutes

Resources
Music selection
Audiotape or CD player
Photocopies of Forms A
and B

Students listen to a popular music selection and fill in words missing from a lyrics sheet. Students with Form A have the answers that students with Form B need and vice versa, so as a follow-up speaking activity, students form pairs and self-check. The class discusses vocabulary, slang, relevant structures, and theme. Having two different cloze forms benefits students by requiring more oral interaction as students check each other.

Procedure

1. Select a song for the activity. Transcribe lyrics and prepare cloze Forms A and B. Each form should have different words missing from the transcribed lyrics.
2. Introduce the music selection by singer, group, and genre, and then have students listen through once for pleasure and to grasp the main idea or context. Ask the students, "How does this song make you feel? What do you think this song is about?"
3. Pass out a cloze exercise Form A or B to each student. Play the recording again and have students fill in the blanks as they listen.
4. Play the selection again, allowing students a second opportunity to fill in the blanks and check their initial responses.
5. Pair students with Form A with students with Form B. Have students check their work by reading the lyrics to each other and providing each other with the missing words and correct spellings. Students must negotiate this task without looking at each other's papers.
6. As a whole class, discuss vocabulary, slang, nonstandard spellings, pronunciation, grammatical structures, and theme.

Caveats and Options

1. When preparing the cloze exercise with the lyrics, blank out every fifth or seventh word or so depending on the pace of the tune. Target lower level vocabulary for Form A and higher level vocabulary for Form B. Pass out the forms according to each student's level of proficiency. The song "Tears in Heaven" by Eric Clapton, for example, is one that works particularly well, because it has clear, discernible lyrics, with a theme.

2. Let the students take ownership of this activity by assigning them, on a rotating basis, responsibility for selecting and providing their favorite music selection. After seeing how it is done, students may even be able to prepare the cloze activity sheets.

3. *Get Cloze With Music* is a great way to introduce a new unit or theme. A unit on homelessness could begin with "Another Day in Paradise" while "Blowing in the Wind" and "Leaving on a Jet Plane" could introduce themes of war or travel. "Tears in Heaven" leads to interesting cross-cultural perspectives on love, death, loss, and the afterlife.

4. *Get Clozer Still:* As a creative writing extension activity, ask students to write the next verse of the song, and then have them share their verses with the class.

5. Do not be surprised, and by all means join in, if students start singing. *Get Cloze With Music* is a pleasurable winding-down activity that tends to draw the whole class together through the universal language of music.

Contributor

Mark Crossman received an MEd in Curriculum and Instruction in TESOL from George Mason University. He teaches K-12 and Adult ESL in Virginia, in the United States.

Top 10 Grammar

Levels
Intermediate; high
school

Aims
Review grammatical
structures
Enhance listening skills

Activity Type
Motivation, application,
or review

Class Time
50 minutes

Preparation Time
2 hours

Resources
Audiotape or CD player
Appropriate songs
recorded on a tape or
compact disc
Handouts

By listening to popular (or all-time-favorite) songs in English, students can revise and better their understanding of grammatical points discussed in class.

Procedure

1. Ask students to listen while you play a song (or part of a song) twice.
2. Have students write down a full sentence (any sentence they can remember) from the song they have just heard.
3. Ask students at random to read their sentences aloud. The teacher or students should write the sentences on the board. Keep all sentences on the board until the end of the activity.
4. Have students identify grammatical structures that occur in these sentences, such as *if* clauses, reported speech, a gerund, or past participles.
5. Next, ask students to identify and write down a sentence that contains a specific grammar point, for example, a preposition, while you play the song for a third time. Repeat Steps 3 and 4.
6. Repeat Steps 1–5 with more songs and more grammatical structures.
7. Hand out the lyrics of the songs you have played and ask students to check the sentences on the board against the lyrics.

Caveats and Options

1. The songs should be sung clearly in English.
2. You may adapt this activity for vocabulary purposes, replacing grammatical structures with vocabulary items.

Wisam Mansour is an assistant professor of English at the Applied Science University in Jordan.

Contributor

Artists in Residence

Levels
Beginning

Aims
Reproduce a drawing
from oral cues
Ask and answer *wh-* and
yes/no questions orally

Activity Type
Application or review

Class Time
30–45 minutes

Preparation Time
5 minutes

Resources
Drawing paper
Crayons, colored
pencils, markers

This activity offers students, through a creative and communicative task, the opportunity to review basic vocabulary topics. Students use art to develop listening and speaking skills.

Procedure

1. Select a vocabulary topic for review, such as the family, the house, sports, or physical characteristics. Review with students a list of relevant vocabulary items.
2. Have students draw a picture that relates to the chosen topic, such as "My Favorite Aunt," "Baseball With My Family," or "My Bedroom." Ask students to include as much detail as possible. For example, "My Bedroom" should show several pieces of furniture with some objects on each piece, and the artist should use color and relative size appropriately.
3. After the artists have finished their work, review with them important structures (e.g., prepositions) and vocabulary (e.g., colors) needed to ask questions about the pictures they will reproduce.
4. Collect the completed pictures, and tape one to each student's back. All artists should wear someone else's picture.
5. Provide students with another sheet of drawing paper, and tell them that their task is to reproduce, as closely as possible, the pictures taped to their backs. To do this, they must ask each other questions and listen carefully to the responses. Students should walk around the room and talk to as many different people as possible.
6. When the artists have finished their reproductions, they should compare them to the pictures they are wearing, and discuss any differences with the artist who drew the original work. As a class, discuss any difficulties that arose in the verbal interaction, such as inaccurate or unclear directions, misuse of prepositions, and so forth.

Caveats and Options.

1. Students who do not like to draw can cut out magazine pictures. Teachers might select magazines in advance according to the topic.
2. To make the creative and linguistic tasks more challenging and interesting, you may require two topics for the picture, such as the family and the house: "My Favorite Aunt in the Living Room." Assuming a very detailed drawing, students would have to comprehend and produce language that deals with physical characteristics, the house, and prepositions. Note, however, that this challenge requires more class time.
3. Pictures that depict actions can be more difficult and time-consuming to draw, but they can also elicit more interesting and varied language, providing more opportunities for language learning.
4. You can extend the oral practice in this activity by having the artists present their pictures, and then take questions from their fellow artists in residence.
5. You can extend the listening practice in this activity by giving each pair of students a drawing that neither artist has seen; one student describes the picture in detail while the other reproduces it.

References and Further Reading

Christison, M.A., & Bassano, S. (1987). *Purple cows and potato chips: Multi-sensory language acquisition activities.* Englewood Cliffs, NJ: Prentice Hall.

Contributor

Albert E. Mussad has taught ESL, and has experience in curriculum and program development. He is the supervisor of world languages and creative arts for Bound Brook, New Jersey public schools in the United States.

Cooperative Construction

Levels
Beginning–intermediate

Aims
Practice pronunciation
Listen to and follow
directions
Work interdependently

Activity Type
Practice

Class Time
15 minutes

Preparation Time
15 minutes (longer the
first time)

Resources
Lego pieces
Preassembled auto and
helicopter
Directions for the auto
(enough for half the
class)
Directions for a
helicopter (enough for
half the class)

This cooperative building activity is geared toward students who learn by doing. It engages every student in the work, encourages pairs to solve a problem, and allows the students to instruct each other.

Procedure

1. Prepare a set of directions for putting together an auto and another set of directions for putting together a helicopter with Legos. (See list of pieces needed and sample directions in Appendix.) Make enough copies of each to pass out to half of the class.

2. Before class, fill sandwich bags with enough Lego parts as needed to make the objects. Prepare one bag for each pair in your class. Make a model auto and helicopter.

3. In class, open a sandwich bag and hold up each Lego piece. Name the piece and write it on the board (e.g., a thin red piece, a six-circle piece, a set of wheels).

4. Pair your students and ask them to sit facing their partners.

5. Tell the pairs that they are going to build a car together. The first student will read the directions. This student must practice pronunciation and is not allowed to touch the Lego pieces. The second student will listen to the directions and put the car together. This student can ask questions but cannot read the directions from the paper. The first student should encourage the second student ("That's right." "Yes, that's good.") and offer praise at the end ("You did it!").

6. As each pair finishes, they should bring their auto to you and compare it to your preassembled model that you have concealed

from view. If their auto is different from the model, explain the step or steps that caused the difference.

7. When all groups are finished, tell the second student to take the car apart and give the pieces to the first student. Give the directions for the helicopter to the second student.

8. Have the pairs repeat the same process but in the opposite role.

9. When the students have finished, collect a sandwich bag with the Lego pieces inside from each pair. Praise the students for their effort and success.

Caveats and Options

1. More advanced students can write their own directions. Ask each pair to put together a car and write directions for how they did it. Then, break up the pairs. Form new partners. Each partner will have the chance to teach the other how to put the auto together.

2. If you do not have Lego pieces, you can use toothpicks, straws, and marshmallows.

References and Further Reading

Kagan, S. (1992). *Cooperative learning*. San Juan Capistrano, CA: Resources for Teachers.

Smith, A., Helming, E., & Mabrey, J. (1990). *Team up: Activities for cooperative learning*. Bloomington, IN: National Educational Service.

Appendix: Sample List and Directions

Twelve Lego pieces needed (colors can be substituted):

one red eight-circle piece
one yellow six-circle piece
one yellow four-circle piece
  with eyes
one red four-circle piece
one blue four-circle piece

two black four-circle pieces
one yellow two-circle piece
one clear two-circle window piece
two sets of wheels
one set of turning helicopter
  blades on a six-circle base

Directions for Making a Car

1. Find the red piece that is eight circles long.
2. Take one set of wheels. Push it under the first two rows in the front.
3. Take the other set of wheels. Push it under Rows 7 and 8 in the back.
4. Take a black four-circle piece and put it over the first two rows.
5. Find the yellow six-circle piece. Place it over Rows 3, 4, and 5 of the red piece.
6. Take the blue four-circle piece and put in over Rows 6 and 7.
7. Pick up the last black four-circle piece and put it behind the blue piece over the eighth row.
8. Take the window piece. Put it over the last yellow row and the first blue row.
9. Find the four-circle piece with the eyes. Put this piece behind the window. The eyes should be near the window.
10. Take the small two-circle piece. Put it behind the piece with the eyes.
11. On the top, place the red piece that is four circles long.
12. You have finished the car. Show it to your teacher.

Directions for Making a Helicopter

1. Find a red piece that is eight circles long.
2. Take one set of wheels. Push it under the first two rows in the front.
3. Take the other set of wheels. Push it under Rows 5 and 6 in the back.
4. Find the yellow six-circle piece. Place it over Rows 1, 2, and 3 of the red piece.
5. Take the blue four-circle piece and place it over Rows 4 and 5 of the red piece.
6. Pick up the small two-circle piece and place it over the sixth row of the red piece.

7. Take a black four-circle piece and put it over Rows 7 and 8 of the red piece.
8. Take the window piece. Put it at the front of the helicopter over the first and second rows of the yellow piece.
9. Find the four-circle piece with the eyes. Put this piece behind the window. The eyes should be near the window.
10. Take the last black four-circle piece. Put it behind the piece with the eyes.
11. Take the six-circle piece with the turning top. Place it over the eyes and black four-circle piece.
12. You have finished the helicopter. Show it to your teacher.

Contributor

Wendy Vicens is a lecturer at the American Language and Culture Program at Arizona State University, in the United States. She is active in materials development and computer-assisted language learning.

Pass the Parsley, Please!

Levels
Intermediate +

Aims
Use practical actions
that have been learned
Give oral directions
completely and
accurately
Demonstrate listening
comprehension by
following directions
accurately

Activity Type
Application

Class Time
25–40 minutes, plus set-
up and clean-up time

Preparation Time
Varies

Resources
Paper plates, cups
Napkins
Eating utensils
Beverages and items of
food

Students in groups of two engage in a lively activity of "elegant" dining that will test two essential and challenging skills of successful communication: giving and carrying out directions precisely. This activity highlights in a humorous way what occurs when these skills are lacking and encourages self-correction of errors as well.

Procedure

1. Design a menu for the luncheon activity, preferably with the students' input. Pair up the students.
2. Bring in all of the items (e.g., food, utensils) yourself or have students be fully or partially responsible for bringing in what is needed. For example, if students are to bring food, divide the class in half and assign each half a different list of food items to bring. Each student should bring enough for two people, because they will be working in pairs and can share those foods with their partners. Some items need to be prepared in advance (peeled, cut, sliced, separated, or spread).
3. Tell one person in each pair to direct the other, step-by-step, in preparing the food (e.g., making a sandwich or cutting up a fruit salad). Eating and drinking the food and beverages must wait until after preparation is complete. Only one direction should be given and carried out at a time.
4. Tell the students that their partners do not know anything about preparing, eating, or drinking these items, and therefore will only do exactly what they tell him or her to do. Then demonstrate the activity for the students, so they see the importance of every direction, by giving one student directions, some of which skip essential steps. For example, "Open the can of peaches. Cut them

into small pieces," misses the step of taking the peaches out of the can, thus demonstrating the difficulty of cutting peaches that are still in the can.

5. Tell the students not to do anything they are not told to do. Often essential directions are omitted, and this becomes obvious only if the listener does not fill in by doing them anyway.

6. Inform the students that every bite of food and every sip of beverage must be indicated through separate commands. The person giving the directions cannot merely say, "Eat the sandwich," but must direct every morsel to be bitten, chewed, and swallowed.

7. Tell the students that when one person has completely finished the allotted food, the partners should reverse roles so both have turns giving and carrying out directions.

8. Circulate to see whether the directions are being given and followed precisely enough. This is to prevent students from only giving a few directions and spending most of the time enjoying eating, but not communicating.

9. Have the students discuss their experiences in carrying out this activity with the whole class.

10. Tell the students what to do to clean up after the activity. Clean-up time can be a continuation of the activity where you and the students collectively give the directions.

Caveats and Options

1. For groups with a more limited vocabulary, be sure that they know sufficient verbs and nouns necessary for carrying out the directions.

2. Part of the fun and humor of the activity is when the direction-giver skips necessary directions and sees the person doing only what was directed, such as: "Pick up the knife. Cut the sandwich. Take a bite of the sandwich." The person, however, is still holding the knife and was not told to put it down nor to pick up the sandwich, which makes taking a bite awkward.

3. Examples of foods that can be used are a sandwich made with several ingredients, such as some kind of a spread: egg salad or tuna salad with lettuce, peanut butter and jelly, cream cheese and jelly; or a fruit salad made from two or three kinds of fruit; or an ice cream

sundae made with different toppings. Beverages can be as simple as water.

4. Choose foods that most people like. Ask ahead of time whether anyone is not able to eat any of the foods you hope to use.

5. Although desks or tables are helpful for the placement of food and utensils, students' laps or the floor can be used with the help of plastic place mats or other suitable coverings.

References and Further Reading

Asher, J. J. (1993). *Learning another language through actions.* (4th ed.). Los Gatos, CA: Sky Oaks Productions.

Larsen-Freeman, D. (1986). *Techniques and principles in language teaching.* Oxford: Oxford University Press.

Contributor

Gertrude Moskowitz is professor of Foreign Language Education at Temple University, in Pennsylvania, in the United States. She teaches methodology, interaction analysis, and multicultural education.

Speak Up—Stand Up

Levels
Any

Aims
Improve pronunciation

Activity Type
Practice or review

Class Time
30 minutes

Preparation Time
10 minutes

Resources
Pronunciation textbook
with minimal pairs
Index cards, box

Students practice oral pronunciation and listening discrimination of minimal pairs with TPR feedback.

Procedure

1. Identify two phonemes the learners are having difficulty distinguishing and select a relevant minimal-pair exercise from the book.

2. Copy the minimal-pair words individually on index cards (each card should have a single word). Place the cards in a box.

3. Introduce Phonemes 1 and 2, demonstrate how the sounds are produced, and give examples by writing words on the board and pronouncing these sounds distinctly. Practice the minimal pairs from the book once through with the class.

4. Select cards from the box at random and pronounce the words. Explain to the students that if they hear Phoneme 1, they should stand up; if they hear Phoneme 2, they should sit down or remain seated. (It is a good idea to arrange the seating so students can stand up without making noise).

5. When it is clear that the majority of the class can hear the difference, invite students in turns to come to the front of the class and pronounce the words from the cards. The class should continue to stand and sit, as appropriate.

6. Depending on the physical response students see, they may wish to try pronouncing their word again.

Caveats and Options

1. Teachers who have access to other native or near-native speakers may wish to use a tape recording of the words, reflecting a variety of accents, instead of reading from the cards.
2. Splitting the class into groups when students start to read cards aloud allows them more opportunities for speaking.

Contributors

David Gardner is a senior language instructor in the English Centre of The University of Hong Kong. Lindsay Miller is an assistant professor in the English Department at City University of Hong Kong.

Dice-y Discussions

Levels
Intermediate +

Aims
Build listening skills and
speaking fluency
Share personal opinions

Activity Type
Motivation, practice, or
review

Class Time
20–30 minutes

Preparation Time
15 minutes

Resources
One die for each pair of
students
Handout of a 6-in. x 6-in.
grid with questions in
each block

This activity promotes short discussions in a gamelike format. Achieving bingo is not the real goal, but the structure allows topics to be discussed randomly, rather than in a predictable sequence.

Procedure

1. Give each student a handout (see Appendix), have students pair up, and give each pair a die.

2. The first student rolls the die, and the number determines the vertical axis. Then, the student rolls again, and the number determines the horizontal axis. The student must speak about the topic in the intersection of the two axes with his or her partner. After having done so, the first student makes an X through that topic on his or her sheet.

3. The second student follows the same procedure.

4. Play continues until one student of the pair gets six Xs in a row in any direction.

5. Students should change partners every 5–10 minutes, and pairs could combine to form groups of four after several pairings.

Caveats and Options

1. Teachers can customize grids for their classes.

2. The game boards can be filled with questions about study topics for review or with "find the error" sentences for grammar practice.

3. You may leave some blocks on the game boards blank for students to add their own topics, or for "free" impromptu questions that they can

ask upon rolling those numbers. Another option is to ask each student to write two (or more) topics or questions they would like to discuss on a card which they hand in the day before, permitting the teacher to choose from these to create the grid.

4. It may be useful to give students guidelines for the discussions, such as: Make one or two statements about the topic, then ask your partner a question about it. The partner should respond. The conversation may extend beyond these two exchanges.

5. For students who complete six conversations in a row on their grid, an option might be to let them choose their own topic or question to pose to their partners, if time remains.

6. This activity should not be used with students who are heavily competitive, because rushing through the discussions for the sake of winning defeats the purpose of the game.

Appendix: Sample Grid

| | Tell Me About . . . |
| | |

	1	2	3	4	5	6
1	what you did last Friday night	a present you have given	a restaurant you like	a news item you heard recently	a funny dream you have had	a job you want to have
2	a movie you have seen recently	a beach you have been to	a pet you have had, or known of	a teacher you have not liked and why	what other languages you speak	the happiest day of your life
3	a place you go when you want to be alone	whether you do your own laundry	a holiday in your native country	how long you have been in the United States	what you read every day	something you wish you could do
4	a present you have received	a time you got lost	whether you are mechanical	what kinds of things you can cook	what time you usually go to bed	a place you would like to go
5	the last time you went to a store	a vacation you have taken	the climate in your native country	something that bothers you	a teacher you liked and why	something you wish you didn't have to do
6	your favorite place to visit	your experience with computers	a person who has influenced your life	an American custom that you find strange	a good friend	a sport you play or have played

Contributor

Elizabeth Bigler taught EFL in Japan and ESL in academic, adult, and refugee programs in Georgia, in the United States. She has an MS in applied linguistics/ESL from Georgia State University.

Pair Shuffle

Levels
Intermediate +

Aims
Interact with multiple
partners
Provide elaborate
rejoinders to oral
questions and
statements

Activity Type
Application or review

Class Time
20-30 minutes

Preparation Time
5 minutes

Resources
None

This activity provides a lively alternative to traditional pair work. Students perform a communicative task in a kinesthetic modality.

Procedure

1. Have students prepare a list of 5-10 questions or statements to share with a partner. These may focus on a grammatical structure (e.g., *How often do you babysit? I have never climbed a mountain.*), a vocabulary unit (e.g., *I like chicken, turkey, and roast beef, but I don't eat pork.*) or a specific topic (e.g., *When did your parents immigrate to the U.S.? Do you think animals should be kept in zoos?*).

2. Ask students to stand in two lines facing each other as partners, and with their list of questions or statements in hand. You may have to participate in this activity so that all students are paired.

3. Explain the shuffle. Students in the first line will ask any question or make any statement from their list to their partner in the second line. These students will respond, and then ask a question or make a statement back to their partners in the first line. Explain "A+" (answer plus) answers. Each time a student responds to a question or statement from a partner, the student must give an additional piece of information, rather than parroting a statement or giving a one word answer. For example, Student 1 asks, "Have you ever written a poem?", and Student 2 answers, "No. **I don't think I could write a good poem; I don't even like to read them.**" Note the "plus" part of the answer in bold. Alternatively, Student 1 makes a statement, "I think O.J. Simpson was guilty because they found his blood at Nicole's house," to which Student 2 responds, "Yeah, I think so because of the **blood and also the glove. They found a glove that fits him.**"

69

4. Tell students that each pair has 1 minute to complete the interaction. When the allotted time has elapsed, you will call "rotate," and the students will move clockwise to the next position so that each student has a new partner. The student standing at the end of the first line moves to the beginning of the second line, and the student at the end of the second line moves over to the first line. This shuffle will be repeated until all students have spoken to each other and have returned to their original partners.
5. Conduct the shuffle. When it is complete, have students share interesting questions, statements, and responses.

Caveats and Options

1. You may have to adjust the time allotted for each interaction to maintain a lively pace; if a single interaction requires more than 1 minute, then the questions or statements posed may require the extended talk available in traditional pair work.
2. Less proficient students may find this fast-paced interaction difficult to manage. You can have them stand by one of the end pairs and tally the numbers of questions and statements posed or write down words or phrases that they hear in the interactions.
3. When students prepare their list of questions and statements, caution them to avoid yes/no questions and simple statements. Encourage them to use *wh-* questions and statements with two propositions, such as "I have never climbed a mountain or traveled to South America." *Wh-* questions and elaborate statements are more interesting and will stimulate an enthusiastic response from the partners. You might want to model questions and statements that use higher order thinking skills for the students.

References and Further Reading

Shoemaker, C.L., & Shoemaker, F.F. (1991). *Interactive techniques for the ESL classroom.* Cambridge, MA: Newbury House.

Contributor

Albert E. Mussad has ESL teaching, curriculum, and program development experience. He is the supervisor of world languages and creative arts for Bound Brook, New Jersey public schools.

English Interview Tape

Levels
Intermediate +; high
school

Aims
Be creative
Use practical English
Converse with a native
or near-native speaker

Activity Type
Motivation

Class Time
Variable

Preparation Time
Variable

Resources
20-minute audiotapes
Tape recorders

This activity encourages students to speak to a native or near-native speaker of English outside the classroom on a specific topic for 10 minutes.

Procedure

1. In class, instruct students on how to prepare an introduction, body, and conclusion for each interview. Ask each student to select a topic and write some related questions. Generate a list of possible topics in class and have students share some of their questions for feedback purposes.

2. Explain to students that before the next class they must interview a native or near native speaker for at least 10 minutes on one of the topics, recording the interview on an audiotape. The interview must have an introduction, body, and conclusion and have natural transitional phrases in between questions as much as possible. Point out to the students that they may make comments or ask additional questions for clarification or explanation if needed, based on the responses of the interviewee.

3. At the next class, collect the tapes and listen to the interviews. Tape your comments on Side B of the students' tapes. This will provide an opportunity for the students to receive the teacher's remarks in a form other than writing. Personalize the comments as much as possible.

Caveats and Options

1. This activity can be adapted for beginners by changing the requirements and making the interview briefer and more basic.
2. You can evaluate the tapes in a number of ways: the quality of the questions and follow-up comments, the number of questions posed and responses given, the fluency or accuracy of the English used by the students.

Contributor

Naoko Tani, an assistant professor at Kwansei Gakuin University in Nishinomiya, Japan has more than 5 years EFL experience. She has an MA in TESOL and an EdM in counseling psychology.

Wat Cha Doin'?

Levels
Intermediate +

Aims
Converse spontaneously
about learned material
Practice using verbs
Be creative

Activity Type
Motivation or practice

Class Time
25–40 minutes

Preparation Time
15–20 minutes +

Resources
Sketches drawn by
teacher
Cards or paper for
student sketches

Using their imagination, students draw simple, original sketches that lead to personalized, spontaneous communication that reviews verbs and other relevant vocabulary. The energy level of students rises as they circulate while conversing and laughing with classmates.

Procedure

1. Draw two sets of three related sketches, with each set illustrating a theme. If you wish to participate in the activity along with the class, draw one or two additional sets of three sketches (see Appendix for sample sketches).

2. If you know your class needs to review verbs to make this activity more effective, prepare a review prior to beginning the activity.

3. Tell the students that if you were not in this classroom with them right now, there is something you would be doing. Ask them to guess what it is from three related sketches you have drawn.

4. Show them a large card (5-in. x 8-in. is a good size) or a sheet of paper on which you have drawn three simple sketches. Tell them that these are clues to help them guess what you would like to be doing.

5. Ask them to identify each sketch first, as a whole group, before guessing what you would like to be doing. Then ask, "What would I like to be doing?"

6. After the students guess the answer, engage them in a conversation on this topic, encouraging them to ask you some questions or make comments related to themselves. Respond to generate a few conversational exchanges with individual students.

7. Take out your second set of sketches and repeat the procedure so the students see how easily conversations can develop from simple sketches.

8. Pass out cards or paper and ask the students what they would be doing if they were not in class right now. Encourage them to be imaginative in their responses. Then ask them to draw three simple sketches as clues to the activity they are representing. Tell them they have 5 minutes to complete the sketches and assure them that the sketches are not expected to be works of art, just as yours were not. Some students will want more time, but speed them along, keeping the drawing time brief because it is the interaction that follows that is important.

9. Tell the students to circulate and communicate with a number of different partners. They should follow the process:
   - guess what the three drawings are
   - guess what the person would like to be doing
   - discuss the subject with the partner.

   After one partner in a pair has had a turn, have students switch roles. When both have had a turn, they find other partners. Give them a specific number of partners to interact with so the class remains lively.

10. Conclude by asking the students what their classmates would like to be doing, and what they learned from the conversations with their partners.

Caveats and Options

1. Dialogues can be short or extended. Allow conversations to develop, but change partners with some frequency because working with different partners and seeing their sketches adds to the fun and interest of the activity.

2. Seeing the sketches students draw is amusing as each person's is different and often unexpected. The sketches add a good deal of interest to the activity, while talking about one's own drawings lends personal appeal.

3. At times, students will compliment each other on their sketches even though they are simple and hastily done.

4. Familiar vocabulary can be reviewed this way as well as verbs, which are the focus. Even if some students choose the same verbs, the sketches will differ, changing the potential for conversation as well.

5. If there is sufficient time to continue this activity, stop the students after they have spoken with about five or six partners, change the question to be answered, and have the students draw another set of three related sketches. This second set of sketches seems to come more easily than the first. The activity can continue with each student presenting new material. Examples of other themes are "Something I'd like to do that I've never done before" or "Something I wish I knew how to do."

6. Word the questions so students practice the desired forms. For example, depending on the wording of the question, the answer called for could be: "I'd like to be skiing," or "I wish I were skiing," or "I wish I knew how to ski."

References and Further Reading

Bassano, S., & Christison, M. A. (1992). *Drawing out: Creative, personalized, whole-language activities.* Englewood Cliffs, NJ: Prentice Hall Regents.

Appendix: Sample Sketches and Potential Dialogues Between Two Students

Dialogue Model

S1: (Looking at Student 2's three sketches) That's a suitcase.

S2: That's right.

S1: And those look like seats—seats on a plane.

S2: Yes, they are.

S1: And that's an airplane.

S2: What about it?

S1: It looks like it's flying.

S2: So what is it I'd like to be doing?

S1: You'd like to be going on a trip?

S2: Yes, but what kind of trip?

S1: A vacation? You'd like to be taking a vacation?

S2: That's it. I'd like to be taking a vacation.

S1: Where would you like to be going?

S2: I'd like to go where it's warm so I can go swimming. What about you?

S1: I'd like to go where it's cold so I can go skiing. Do you ski?

S2: No, but I'd like to learn. It's your turn. Let me see your drawings.

Dialogue Model

S2: (Continues after looking at the sketches) That's a chair. And PC. What is PC?

S1: It's something you eat that starts with those letters.

S2: Oh, popcorn! And that's a movie screen.

S1: So what would I like to be doing?

S2: You'd like to be seeing a movie.

S1: Yes, I'd like to be going to a movie.

S2: What kinds of movies do you like?

S1: I like mysteries and scary movies.

S2: You're brave! I like movies that are funny.

Contributor

Gertrude Moskowitz is professor of Foreign Language Education at Temple University in Pennsylvania, in the United States. She teaches methodology that emphasizes humanistic teaching.

Garden Cameras

Levels
Beginning-intermediate;
middle school

Aims
Develop observation
skills
Practice working with a
partner
Share information orally
in a group
Appreciate the five
senses
Empathize with the
blind

Activity Type
Practice or motivation

Class Time
30 minutes

Preparation Time
None

Resources
None

This activity leads students outdoors for an active break from regular classroom procedures. If your school has a garden, that is the ideal setting, but any outdoor area with a variety of things to see and talk about would work.

Procedure

1. Discuss the five senses, reviewing what each one does and how they interact. Ask students to focus on the sense of sight. Discuss how a photograph is the same or different from what we actually see (or think we see). Show photos of the classroom for comparison, if possible.
2. Explain the activity. "Today we are going outside to focus on our sense of sight and observe carefully the things in one area. Then we will describe them."
3. Demonstrate the activity with a pair of students. Explain that one will be the photographer, and the other will be the camera. They will be trying to describe objects or scenes fully, using descriptive language.
   - Tell the camera to close his or her eyes. The photographer focuses the camera by pointing that student at a picture or special subject. The camera must keep his or her eyes shut tightly until the photographer exposes the picture by lightly pressing on the camera's shoulder.
   - The camera then opens his or her eyes and observes carefully what is directly in front of him or her for a slow count of four by the photographer. The camera then closes the eyes and describes the scene to the photographer in as much detail as possible. The photographer agrees, disagrees, or adds to the description.
   - The camera keeps his or her eyes closed while the photographer points him or her at another picture.

4. Divide the class into pairs. Let them decide who will be the camera first and who will be the photographer. Tell students they will be taking three pictures, then switching roles.

5. Take the class outside. Have each photographer take three pictures and then switch roles with the cameras. Circulate to help with procedures and descriptions.

6. As the pairs complete their task, have them gather in groups of six and have each describe their favorite picture from their point of view as the camera.

7. Return to class after groups have shared. Lead a discussion about how the students felt as cameras with their eyes closed and being moved about by someone else. Ask questions like, "What sense do you use the most?" "Can you name something you looked at that made you feel good?" "Could you focus on just one item or did you see a lot of items?" "Can you name something that made you feel bad?"

8. Discuss what it would be like to be blind. Tell students about seeing-eye dogs, the Braille writing system, and libraries with talking books for the blind.

Caveats and Options

1. If any students are not familiar with cameras, show them one prior to beginning this activity, and explain how it works. Teach the vocabulary: *photographer, camera, shutter, lens, focus, exposure (expose)*.

2. To integrate art, discuss how paintings differ from photographs or what we actually see. Bring in paintings to compare. Have students paint or draw a picture of their favorite scene from the activity.

3. If students have a problem touching someone on the shoulder, this activity should not be used.

References and Further Reading

Jaffe, R., & Appel, G. (1990). *The growing classroom: Garden-based science*. Menlo Park, CA: Addison-Wesley.

Contributor

Joan M. Dungey has taught ESL at all levels. She is the curriculum coordinator at Yellow Springs High School and teaches in the languages and literature department at Cedarville College and in the education department at the MacGregor School of Antioch University in Ohio, in the United States.

Easily Into the Summary

Levels
Intermediate; middle
school

Aims
Develop summary skills
through oral practice

Activity Type
Review

Class Time
45 minutes

Preparation Time
5–15 minutes

Resources
Texts from students'
other school subjects,
especially humanities

Learners, when first faced with summarizing, often believe that task is too difficult. This activity reassures learners and encourages them to summarize everyday information to their classmates by reporting what they have seen, heard, or done, and then to practice this skill with school texts.

Procedure

1. Choose a reading passage from the students' textbook for later use in this activity.

2. Ask students to bring the chosen text to class.

3. As a warm-up, ask students a question allowing expression of personal experience that is relevant to your class, such as:

   ● What did you do last night/weekend?

   ● Who watched _____ [film] last night/last week? What happened in it?

   ● What lesson have you just studied? What did you learn?

   Encourage short responses that elicit facts without elaborate description or detail. Using body language, indicate when answers are getting longer than desired, but do not specifically say you want students to summarize or make other comments that might suggest a formality to the activity. Note the responses briefly on the board, particularly if they are lengthy. Orally, draw together the different responses in a sentence or two, such as "Last weekend this class (a)___, (b)___, (c)___, (d)___, and (e)___."

4. Pair students and designate one in each pair A, the other B. Tell those in Group A to describe an incident from their lives. Decide in advance what sort of incident would be stimulating to your students:

The day I got into trouble; A time that I was really frightened; The most difficult thing I've ever done. Instruct the students as follows: "How much can you tell your partner about [the topic] in 3 minutes? You must not stop talking!" Have pairs begin and be very strict about time.

5. Then ask pairs to combine into groups of four (or more, depending on class size and dynamics). Tell the Bs from each pair to report what the speaker said to the group, but restrict the time to 15 seconds. The groups provide an audience for the retelling and a chance for individuals to tell each other how well they think their story has been represented and to compare experiences.

6. Afterwards, draw comments from the whole class about these three functions: (a) telling as much as you can about a topic; (b) reducing the information for retelling it; and (c) making sense of what was retold.

7. Place students in the same pairs again. Tell those in Group B to think of an everyday object (or give the pupils a prompt card naming an object) and describe it to their partner in one sentence. The A partner, in turn, must decide what is being described. Descriptions could be in terms of appearance, function, and so on. Then discuss as a class whether this task was difficult to do with just one sentence. After the discussion, ask some students to try again with the whole class.

8. As a result of these activities, elicit from students what characteristics make the description easy to understand, such as length (Is a longer or a shorter description better? Is this always the case?), accuracy, specific detail, and other factors.

9. Having established some criteria, continue with an activity in which students tell each other, in pairs, about a film they have seen, a book they have read, or a favorite television show. Preferably this should be something with a plot, to practice retelling the story without superfluous detail. Allow 2 minutes for the first partner, 3 minutes for discussion, then 2 minutes for the other partner to take a turn.

10. Turn to the chosen passages from a textbook. Assign a passage to each partner and give pairs an appropriate amount of time to read,

then stop them. Ask them to tell their partners in 2 minutes what their passage was about. At the end of this activity, encourage the partners to discuss what happened and give feedback to the class.

Caveats and Options

1. In these early stages, take the focus off the teacher as audience. Explain that the audience is a friend. Subsequent activities might be introduced as "Your friend has not read this passage. Tell him or her what it's about," leading to "Your friend in ____ [another place] has not read this. Write and tell him or her what it was about."

2. Choose textbook passages that are substantial enough for Step 9 to be a demanding activity so that students are fully engaged in the task.

3. Students' work may not be entirely accurate at this stage. Address their errors or omissions in later lessons, pointing out how to identify key points of information. For this lesson, focus on oral summaries in a nonthreatening manner.

4. If the activity described here is too long for one lesson, be selective with the steps or do it over two lessons. Make the tasks relevant to your students by developing activities that deal with their life experiences and that they can describe informally to a friend.

5. As a follow-up activity in a later lesson, ask students to write what they told their partners in Step 6 above.

6. In schools that do not have generous supplies of English textbooks, or where class sizes are very big, you can make use of whatever materials are available. Use of this activity can be part of an overall language across the curriculum policy. The reading passages can be taken from textbooks or other materials for subjects across the curriculum, though preferably in the target language (in this case English), to provide authenticity.

References and Further Reading

Bevan, R. (1992). *Secondary English for Namibia, Book 1.* Harlow, England: Longman.

Carter, R. (Ed). (1990). *Knowledge about language and the curriculum: The LINC reader.* London: Hodder & Stoughton.

Gillham, B. (1990). *The language of school subjects*. London: Heinemann.
Nuttall, C. (1982). *Teaching reading skills in a foreign language*. London: Heinemann.

Contributors

Rex Berridge, teacher educator and former English Language Adviser with the British Council, works at the English Language Unit, University of Wales Aberystwyth, in the United Kingdom. Jenny Muzambindo, teacher educator and expert in English teaching and the methodology of teaching across the curriculum, is head of Communication Skills at Gweru Teachers College, in Zimbabwe.

Poetry Alive!

Levels
Any

Aims
Practice pronunciation
and intonation skills
Practice speaking before
a group
Enjoy literature in small
segments

Activity Type
Application

Class Time
Two–six class periods

Preparation Time
1-2 hours

Resources
10-20 books of poetry
that the students can
peruse
Handouts of single
poems
Evaluation criteria
sheets

In this activity, students enjoy applying a familiar skill (memorization) while practicing other skills (oral presentations, poetic interpretation) that can be difficult or scary.

Procedure

1. Assemble books of poetry and prepare handouts of single poems for the students to read over.
2. Before the activity, prepare a list of questions students can use in their groups for Step 7 of the procedure. Sample questions are
   - Are there any words in this poem that you don't understand?
   - Can you help me say this word?
   - Do you know the meaning of this word?
   - Will you listen to me read my poem?

   You may formulate questions and distribute to the students or ask the class to brainstorm questions and write them on the board.
3. Have each student select a poem from the resources provided. This is a time-consuming process because students need to look through books and/or handouts to pick out one they are comfortable with. By carefully choosing the poetry books, specifying pages in the books, or providing handouts to look through, you can limit the levels of difficulty and types of poems. This step can take an entire class period.
4. Approve the students' choices. This step will prevent two or more students from choosing the same poem or more advanced students from choosing a poem that is obviously very easy.
5. Have students copy the poem exactly as it is printed. This copying of the words will be the first step in the internalization process and

will help students become aware of the different shapes and sizes that poems come in. Check the copying for accuracy in every detail.

6. Tell the students to reread their poems and underline words that may be difficult to pronounce or understand.

7. Have students continue becoming familiar with the poem by writing definitions for words, asking for help from fellow students or the teacher on pronunciation, and writing the meaning of the line, verse, or the entire poem. Beginning students will do less poetic interpretation than advanced students. The students can continue to work on Step 6 at home.

8. In pairs or triads, have students practice reading the poem aloud. They should discuss unfamiliar vocabulary and the meaning of the poem in general. The students should use the list of questions from the resource section during this step.

9. Move from group to group to listen to the oral readings and discussion and to correct pronunciation and grossly incorrect interpretations.

10. Have students take home their poems for further work and memorization.

11. Give the students the criteria on which their presentations will be graded and go over each one so that the students understand what is expected. Point out that audience behavior is included in the criteria. (See sample in Appendix.)

12. Have students re-form their groups to practice their presentations and obtain feedback from group members based on the criteria.

13. The students can take home their poems for further work and memorization if necessary.

14. Have students present their poems to the class. Using the criteria, assess each student as each poem is presented.

Caveats and Options

1. Spend the time in class discussing all the steps with the students in advance. Once they understand each step, one or more steps may be assigned for homework.

2. The teacher's role for the first six steps is one of facilitator. The teacher will be unable to give extensive help in pronunciation until all the students have chosen and copied their poems. Therefore,

when students reach Step 6, encourage them to work on their own as much as possible.

3. At times, the whole class can be assigned the same poem if the students are at about the same level and are experiencing a similar pronunciation or grammar problem.

4. Students can sometimes present poems from their culture in their first language with an English translation or summary.

5. Students can present songs they like from their culture or that of the United States.

6. Encourage beginning students to select poems that are simple so that they can work primarily on pronunciation and presentation.

7. The tension of the presentation process may be alleviated by asking for volunteers.

8. The activity can be extended for advanced students by adding lessons about poetic meter and form and literary devices used in poetry.

References and Further Reading

A swinger of birches. *Poems by Robert Frost for young people.* (1982). Owings Mills, MD: Stemmer House.

I'm nobody! Who are you? *Poems by Emily Dickinson for young people.* (1978). Owings Mills, MD: Stemmer House.

Ciardi, J. (1961). *I met a man.* Boston: Houghton Mifflin.

Ciardi, J. (1962). *You read to me, I'll read to you.* New York: J.B. Lippincott.

Ghigna, C. (1994). *Tickle day: Poems from Father Goose.* New York: Hyperion Books for Children.

Koch, K., & Farrell, K. (1985). *Talking to the sun.* An illustrated anthology of poems for young people. New York: Henry Holt /Metropolitan Museum of Art.

Silverstein, S. (1974). *Where the sidewalk ends.* New York: Harper & Row.

Silverstein, S. (1981). *A light in the attic.* New York: Harper & Row.

Appendix: Evaluation Criteria for Poem Presentation

Criteria	Points		
	1	2	3
Volume	Unable to hear	Only those in front can hear	Loud enough for all to hear
Intonation	Monotone voice	Some inflection used	Strong attempt at appropriate inflection
Posture	Body leaning	Body straight but stiff	Body straight, relaxed
Eye contact	No eye contact	Some eye contact	Frequent eye contact
Audience behavior	Did other school work or socialized	Watched speaker most of the time	Watched speaker all of the time
Pronunciation	Less than 60% correct	65% to 80% correct	85% to 100% correct

Write mispronounced words here:

Contributor

Lyn Froning has taught ESL at the middle and high school level for 25 years in American Samoa, and in Maryland, Hawaii, Massachusetts, and Alabama, in the United States.

Fabulous Oral Presentations: The Metacognitive Approach

Levels
Intermediate +

Aims
Improve oral
presentation skills
Increase confidence
about public speaking
Develop metacognitive,
self-evaluative
processing skill

Activity Type
Application

Class Time
2–4 hours for initial
brainstorming, self
evaluation, and
modeling
6 minutes per student
for oral presentations
and feedback at regular
intervals thereafter

Preparation Time
1–2 hours

Resources
Videotaping equipment
(optional)

This activity, a structured, proven alternative to the hit-or-miss approach to oral reports, enables students to recognize their oral presentation strengths, develop strategies to correct weaknesses, gain confidence in public speaking, and inform one another about topics of interest. The activity works best when embedded in thematic units, giving students authentic purposes for communicating information at regular intervals in a richly contextualized environment.

Procedure

(Steps 1–5 are done only the first time through.)

1. Set the stage by facilitating a brainstorming session on questions such as these:
   - Why are oral presentation skills important?
   - When might these skills be helpful to us?
   - What kinds of careers require good oral presentation skills?
2. Have the students do a guided freewrite about an experience they have had with oral presentations, answering questions such as these:
   - Who gave the oral presentation? When? Where? For what purpose? Who was the audience?
   - Was the presentation successful? Why or why not?
3. Model two oral presentations. The first should be an example of an unsuccessful presentation. For example, read rather than interact, mumble, chew gum, fumble with your graphic aids, use graphic aids that are messy and confusing, turn your back to the audience, mispronounce key words, and so on. (This should be a funny moment! Ham it up!) Debrief the first model by having students generate a list of "Oral Presentation Pitfalls." Second, model a successful presentation and debrief.

4. Next, brainstorm a list of "Keys to Fabulous Oral Presentations." Use a T-Chart organizer (see Appendix A) for this debriefing. Label the left side of the chart *Desirable Behaviors* and the right side *Steps in Preparation*. After you and the students list the desirable behaviors on the left side, ask the students what they think you did to ensure that these desirable behaviors were in place. Add these to the right side. This chart becomes the basis for the self-evaluation form that the class can create. (See Appendix B for a sample self-evaluation form that my students and I devised.)

5. Have the students do a guided freewrite on the steps they usually take to prepare for oral presentations.

6. Hand out an oral presentation self-evaluation form. Have students complete this form individually and then discuss it with a partner. Tell each student to select an improvement goal and outline steps to reach the goal. Confer with students about their goals.

7. Several times during the year, usually once per thematic unit, have the students give oral presentations. Ask them to begin their presentations by identifying their goal for improvement and the steps they have taken to reach that goal. After their reports, solicit feedback from their classmates and provide some yourself regarding the progress they have made in reaching their goal, and other areas in which they have done particularly well.

8. Hold conferences with students periodically to ensure that they are moving forward along their path toward proficiency as public speakers.

Caveats and Options

1. It is important to model for students the type of feedback that is helpful after oral presentations.

2. Some classes benefit from videotaping these presentations. During the year, the students' tapes of their oral presentations can become a helpful part of their portfolio.

Appendix A: T-Chart

Keys to Fabulous Oral Presentations	
Desirable Behaviors	*Steps in Preparation*
1. Speak slowly and clearly	Practice in front of the mirror. Practice with a friend or parent. Tape record yourself.
2. Organize your notes and visual aids.	Mark the pages with post-its. Write main ideas on cards. Tape up visuals first.
3. Look at everybody, not just one or two people. Don't read!	Practice with friends. Practice with a mirror.
4. Make the main idea clear in the beginning.	Check with a partner after the first minute of a practice presentation.
5. Do something interesting—tell a joke, bring food, use pictures.	Ask yourself, "How can I spice it up?"
6. Don't mumble. Don't shout.	Practice with a friend.

Appendix B: Sample Self-Evaluation Form for Fabulous Oral Presentations

Name: Date:

Rank your skills in the following areas. 1 = very weak to 5 = very strong. For every area that you mark 3 or lower, write one or two specific steps you could take to improve that skill.

1. I prepare my oral presentations so clearly that my audience understands the topic I am going to discuss within the first few seconds.

   1   2   3   4   5

   Steps I could take to improve:

2. I relate my topic to other ideas or experiences that I know my audience understands, and I always include examples of the most important points.

   1   2   3   4   5

   Steps I could take to improve:

3. My pronunciation is clear.

   1   2   3   4   5

   Steps I could take to improve:

4. My rate of speech is just right; not too fast or too slow.

   1   2   3   4   5

   Steps I could take to improve:

5. My tone of voice is loud enough and interesting.

   1   2   3   4   5

   Steps I could take to improve:

6. I look at and speak to my audience. I do not read my speech.

   1   2   3   4   5

   Steps I could take to improve:

7. I select or prepare visual aids that are attractive and interesting.

    1   2   3   4   5

    Steps I could take to improve:

8. I touch the audience's senses with music, food, art, or experiences when it would be helpful to do so.

    1   2   3   4   5

    Steps I could take to improve:

9. I use humor when I can.

    1   2   3   4   5

    Steps I could take to improve:

10. I communicate interest in and excitement about my topic.

    1   2   3   4   5

    Steps I could take to improve:

Now go back and select the first area you will work to improve. Be sure you have at least two specific steps you will take to improve in this area. Discuss this goal with your learning partner and your teacher. All three of you will sign below when your goal and your plans for reaching your goal are clear.

(student)

(partner)

(teacher)

Contributor

Margaret A. Dwyer taught high school ESL for many years and now works in teacher preparation in the MATESOL Program at Teachers College, Columbia University, in New York, in the United States.

◆ Developing Language Through Reading

Double Entry Reading Logs: A Reading, Thinking, Writing Connection

Levels
High beginning +

Aims
Evaluate understanding
of a text
Respond personally, in
writing, to what is read

Activity Type
Practice

Class Time
One or two 45-minute
periods

Preparation Time
30–60 minutes

Resources
One reading log
notebook per student

Here is an interesting way to get students to think about what they read and to encourage them to respond personally to reading assignments. Regular use of this method helps students understand and remember difficult reading material and can also allow for meaningful class discussions.

Procedure

1. Before asking students to use this method for the first time, spend about 30–60 minutes practicing it yourself.
2. Have students fold a page in half (vertically) in their reading log and then unfold it so that there is a line down the middle of the page.
3. Ask students to read an assignment and stop at the end of each paragraph or small identifiable section (depending on the difficulty of the reading material). Have students ask themselves, "What did I just read?" and then write their understanding of that section on the left side of the page.
4. On the right side of the page, ask the students to write things they do not understand or things they want to ask about. They may have questions or opinions about what they have read or there may be vocabulary words that are confusing to them. This process can be hard for students at first if they are not normally asked to think about

what they do not know. Students usually do not have a hard time identifying difficult vocabulary words, but asking them to write their own questions is not as easy. As an incentive, you can give additional points to students who write their own questions or opinions about their reading.

5. Use the material students have written on the right side of the page as the focus of that day's lesson. Walk around the class, scanning the right side of the students' pages and marking words to discuss that day. Ask students to write those words on the board. Then review the reading with the students and discuss the difficult words that students have identified.

6. Initially, students will ask few questions in their logs. As you scan what students have written, mark interesting questions that you want the class to discuss. Have students with marked questions write them on an overhead transparency and then place the questions on a projector for the class to consider. These questions can serve as models for the type of questions other students can write.

7. After a reading passage has been discussed, ask students to write about what they learned from a reading or what they would like to remember. This becomes a "learning log" that students write on a blank, unfolded page in their reading log books. This is a good way to get students to put together everything they have read and discussed. It is also a good way for the teacher to evaluate how much the students are learning.

Caveats and Options

1. Sheets of lined paper stapled into a manila folder offer an inexpensive alternative to journal notebooks.

2. Students who are used to writing answers to a list of questions about a text may be intimidated by this activity at first. After a little practice, though, they are often surprised at how much they can write about what they have learned. The important idea in Step 2 is that the students are writing what they understand, not trying to guess the "correct answer" that the teacher expects. I encouraged my students to do this by reading a paragraph with them. Then I told them to write their understanding of the section in their own words. As I circulated, I read what each student wrote and told the student that

the writing was 100% correct. I explained that because they were writing what they understood, they could not write the wrong thing.

3. Grading: I give an initial grade of a minus (−), check (✓), or plus (+) for each reading log. A minus is for logs that were begun but not finished. A check is for logs that appeared finished but have no questions on the right side. A plus is for logs with inference questions or opinions on the right side. Later I convert these to points (minus = 3; check = 4; plus = 5). These points quickly add up because of the many reading logs that students are assigned.

4. Vocabulary Lists: I sometimes ask students to choose five new words they want to learn and to write them (along with a definition and a sentence) in a vocabulary section in the back of their reading logs. Because each student will have a different set of words, for testing they list their own words on a sheet of paper that is turned in to me the day before a quiz. Then the following day, the paper is returned for them to write a sentence for each word they have selected.

5. After doing logs for a month or two, my students often ask more questions than we can answer in a class period. As an alternate activity, I sometimes ask students to discuss their questions in groups and then ask the students to select one or two questions that they want to discuss with the whole class.

6. Initially, I told students that I expected them to write their understanding of a text in their own words. In using this method myself, however, I found that it was sometimes more efficient to copy sections of the text rather than to try to rephrase it. In a teacher research project in which I studied my students as they worked through this process, I found that students who copied sentences from the text learned the material as well as those who rephrased important ideas into their own words. The important skill students needed to learn was how to identify the most important sentences rather than copy whole paragraphs. Because this activity was about reading comprehension and not about summarizing, selected copying made sense.

7. Some students seem to have little understanding of what they are reading. Students who appear to understand parts of a reading but miss the big picture have additional opportunities to learn the

material. The rephrasing of the reading that occurs as the class discusses difficult vocabulary words sometimes helps promote better understanding. Also, discussion of the students' questions can prompt more questions that help clarify a reading.

8. Students need to have reached a certain level of language competence in order to feel comfortable with this method. If students at a high beginning level have difficulty with it, I usually allow individual students to do the more traditional type of activity, answering prepared questions while I work individually with them to help them build the self-confidence they need to do this activity. I let them tell me when they think they are ready to write their double entry logs along with the rest of the class.

References and Further Reading

Berthoff, A. (1988). *Forming, thinking, writing: The composing imagination.* (2nd ed.) Montclair, NJ: Boynton/Cook.

Contributor

Joseph C. Bellino is an ESOL teacher at Montgomery Blair High School, in Maryland, in the United States, and a teacher consultant for the Maryland Writing Project.

...ng to Summarize

This activity teaches students how to summarize using a graphic organizer. It may be used as practice or assessment of students' reading and summary writing skills. A good supplement to any curriculum, this enjoyable activity gives students exposure to authentic U.S. texts.

Practice writing summaries
Improve reading comprehension skills
Reinforce connection between reading and writing

Activity Type
Practice or assessment

Class Time
40–50 minutes

Preparation Time
15–20 minutes

Resources
The Reader's Digest, Cobblestone, Calliope, or readings from textbooks
Graphic organizer chart(s)

Procedure

1. For the first step, teach students how to summarize. This can be done by utilizing a variation of *GRASP* (Guided Reading and Summarizing Procedure).
   - Teacher selects the same article for each student to read silently.
   - After reading the article, students turn it face down on their desks.
   - Teacher presents and explains the graphic organizer (see Appendix A).
   - Students then work together as a class (or in small groups) with teacher guidance to fill in the organizer appropriately. The teacher has the option of having students recall the text from memory or having them refer to it as they complete the organizer.
   - Students take the information from the graphic organizer and write it in prose form, thus completing the summary (see Appendix B).
2. The next step involves students working through this process independently. They either select a teacher-approved article (good sources for this include *Reader's Digest, Cobblestone,* and *Calliope)* or a reading in a textbook from another content area.
3. Students may then exchange summaries and try to fit their classmate's prose back into the graphic organizer format. They can compare the new version with the original completed organizers.

Caveats and Options

1. A variation on this activity is to assign article- or text-summaries as homework (e.g., one or two summaries per week).
2. Another option is to have students select readings in textbooks from other classes to integrate multiple content areas.
3. After students become comfortable with the process, they can select their own reading material (with approval from the teacher). The activity can then be used as an independent in-class task.

References and Further Reading

Hayes, D. A. (1989). Helping students GRASP the knack of writing summaries. *Journal of Reading, 33*, 96–101.

Appendix A: Sample Graphic Organizer for Summarizing

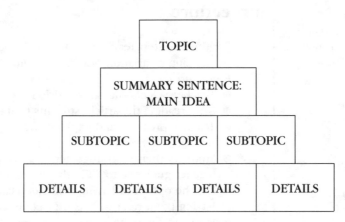

Appendix B: Sample Student Organizer

dogs and dise-ases

Why does many pedigre-ed dogs have genetic diseases

AKC

breeders

peoples that doesn't want no mutts

hereditary weakness

breeder education

puppy lemon laws

proves pedigree, not health

Pedigreed dogs have lots of genetic diseases, but why? Because of AKC and breeders and peoples that doesn't want no mutts. AKC proves pedigree, not health. Breeders need education so they don't make hereditary weakness on dogs. Puppy lemon laws help to.

Sample student organizer based on Lemonick, M. D. (1995, April). What have we done to man's best friend? *Reader's Digest*, 60–64.

Contributors

Ellen Bartsch teaches in the Curriculum Department at McPherson College in Kansas, in the United States. Carolyn Kaltenbach teaches English in Japan.

Hall of Fame/Hall of Shame

Levels
Any

Aims
Read a newspaper
Express an opinion
orally and in writing
Negotiate
Build consensus
Work cooperatively

Activity Type
Practice

Class Time
60–90 minutes

Preparation Time
None

Resources
Newspapers, newsprint
or poster paper
Scissors
Color markers
Instruction sheet
Sample poster

Working in cooperative groups, students skim the newspaper to locate three examples of people or events for the Hall of Fame and three for the Hall of Shame. Each group creates a poster display and makes a presentation to the class explaining their choices and how their group achieved consensus.

Procedure

1. Provide background knowledge by discussing sections of the newspaper, what kind of people or events make the news, the meanings of fame, shame, and rank. Explain the instructions (see Appendix for instruction sheet) and student roles in cooperative groups and show a sample finished poster.

2. Form cooperative groups of three or four students, allowing students to choose roles that match their level of proficiency and learning style, such as materials person, scribe, cut-and-paster, presenter.

3. Distribute materials and monitor groups as they discuss their selections. Check for understanding and model group processing skills, asking such questions as: Where is this person going? In the Hall of Fame or the Hall of Shame? What was your reason? Did everyone agree on that? What does ___ (student name) think? What does ___ (point to word) mean?

4. After teams have had sufficient time to prepare their posters, call on each group to present their results. Discuss similarities and differences among the groups' choices and reasons.

Caveats and Options

1. Choose a newspaper that is more comprehensible for English language learners, such as *USA Today* or *News For You.*
2. You may use the same edition of the paper for all groups or different editions. Providing each group with a separate edition of the newspaper leads to greater variety during whole-class presentations, while using the same edition leads to discussion of how placement in the Hall of Fame/Hall of Shame of the same selection of individuals or events varies from group to group.
3. Students may create two columns on their poster displays, one for the Hall of Fame and one for the Hall of Shame, or create separate posters for each.
4. Recycle this activity on a regular basis. Once familiar with the structure and the task, students will find a fresh newspaper provides a wealth of new language and stimulus for new discussion.

References and Further Reading

Kagan, S. (1992). *Cooperative learning.* San Juan Capistrano, CA: Kagan Cooperative Learning.

News For You. (Published by New Readers Press, a division of Laubach Literacy International. Available by writing to Box 131, Syracuse, NY 13210 USA, or by phoning 800-448-8878 [in North America] or 315-422-9121 from outside North America)

West, A. (1994). *Speaking of language: Using the newspaper in ESL studies.* Overland Park, KS: News Relief. (An activity guide available from News Relief, Inc., 11624 Grant Drive, Overland Park, KS 66210 USA)

Appendix: Instructions for Hall of Fame/Hall of Shame Posters

1. For the Hall of Shame: Look through your newspaper and either select three people who have done shameful deeds, or select three events that are shameful.
2. For the Hall of Fame: Select three people who have done good deeds, or three events that deserve our admiration.
3. Cut out a picture or a headline or an article for each person (or event) you have chosen and arrange them on your poster.
4. As a team, decide who deserves the most shame and the most fame. Rank your selections 1–3, 1 being the most shameful or most

deserving of fame. Label and decorate your poster display. Write an explanation of your selections next to each one.

5. Prepare to present your poster to the class. Be ready to explain the reasons for your group's selections and the order in which you have ranked them.

Contributor

Mark Crossman received an MEd in Curriculum and Instruction in TESOL from George Mason University and teaches K-12 and Adult ESL in Virginia, in the United States.

News and Views

Levels
High beginning-
intermediate; high
school

Aims
Gain experience in
reading for information
Practice reading and
responding to
nonfiction
Learn about and discuss
current events
Take notes

Activity Type
Practice or application

Class Time
50-60 minutes

Preparation Time
30 minutes

Resources
Copies of newspaper
articles

Student groups read a news article and take notes on it. The groups then present their articles with one student introducing the article and telling the main idea, and then others in the group adding details.

Procedure

1. Read and choose several news articles that will interest the students. The articles should be long enough to provide sufficient information for several students to present.
2. Circle the articles on the newspapers that you are assigning each group. Each group should read a different article.
3. Divide the class into groups of three or four students.
4. Distribute the newspapers with the assigned articles to the class. Tell the students to:
   ● carefully read the article; students typically take turns, each reading a paragraph or two aloud
   ● take notes individually about the article; one group member writes down the main idea or theme of the article
   ● (the remaining group members) take turns recording other information and details from the article
   ● prepare to present the article to the class as a group
5. Allow 20-30 minutes for students to read their article and take notes on it.
6. Have the groups present. One student introduces the article and explains the main idea or information expressed. The other group members then take turns presenting additional information about the article from the notes they have taken. The other groups follow in turn.

Caveats and Options

1. Classmates can ask questions about an article after a group has reported.
2. Some groups might want to report on their news articles by role-playing radio or television broadcasters.
3. I have used this activity with *News For You*, a news weekly available in class sets. *News for You* is a short newspaper with articles and editorials that are appropriate for high school ESL students.

References and Further Reading

News For You. (Published by New Readers Press, a division of Laubach Literacy International. Available by writing to Box 131, Syracuse, NY 13210 USA, or by phoning 800-448-8878 [in North America] or 315-422-9121 [outside North America])

Contributor

Marlene M. Ryder (BA and MEd in languages and teaching) teaches high school ESL in Virginia, in the United States, and has taught French and Spanish at university and secondary levels.

What Happens Next?

Levels
Intermediate +; middle school

Aims
Enjoy reading literature in English and listening to stories
Practice writing

Activity Type
Motivation

Class Time
30–40 minutes

Preparation Time
10–20 minutes

Resources
Copies of the same book for each student

This activity stimulates students' interest in English literature by presenting material in a nonthreatening manner. It brings to the forefront the content of the story rather than the vocabulary or grammar.

Procedure

This particular lesson introduces the students to Golding's (1958) *The Lord of the Flies,* but the steps can be applied to other books.

1. Ask students to place a sheet of paper and a pen in front of them on the desk.
2. Inform students that you are going to tell them a story. Tell them to sit back and make themselves comfortable, close their eyes, and just listen.
3. Ask them to imagine that they are small children about 9 or 10 years old. They have been taken from their parents to an airport to be sent away from their country because there is danger. They are too young to understand what is happening.
4. Continue by telling them how they have been flying for about 3 hours, which seems like a long time to a child. There are a lot of other children on the plane, but they are not talking to each other because none of them know each other.
5. Stop and ask students to open their eyes and write five or six sentences quickly about how they think they would feel in this situation.
6. When the students have finished, tell them to sit back, get comfortable again, and close their eyes.
7. Continue the story: They have been flying for some time and suddenly the plane seems to be doing strange things. It is out of

control and falling towards the earth! They don't know what is happening. The plane crashes, but they are not hurt. Somehow they are still alive and can move. They get out of the wreckage and look around. They are on a beach. They think they might be on an island but they do not know. They cannot see another person.

8. Tell students to open their eyes again and quickly write what they are thinking and feeling. If they seem to be a little slow starting, you could ask leading questions (e.g., "Are you frightened?" "Do you wish there was somebody with you?").

9. Let the students write for a few minutes and then ask them to describe what they can see with the eyes of their imagination. Again some guidance could be useful (e.g., "Are there trees?" "Can you see any animals?" "Is there a field?"). After students have written for about 3 minutes, tell them to put their pens down, sit back, and close their eyes again.

10. Continue the story: You are walking around the wreckage of the plane and are feeling very frightened. You do not like being alone and you very much want somebody to come and take control but there does not seem to be anybody around. You are very confused. What is going to happen? Suddenly you hear a voice. You cannot see anybody but you can hear them. They are calling.

11. Stop and ask the students if they want to know what happens next. Explain that you have been telling them the beginning of a story about a group of boys whose plane has crashed and that the story goes on to tell about their adventures.

12. Read the opening chapter of the book or part of it to the students. Do not read too much, just enough to whet their appetites and then tell them to continue reading the book at home.

13. To maintain interest in the text and lessen the task for slower readers, put the students into groups and have each group responsible for reading a section of the text and then reporting back to the class about what happened in their section. This should not preclude the students from reading all the chapters, but does allow those who are slower readers to follow all of the story.

14. You could also put a "Character Chart" or an "Adventure Chart" on the wall in the classroom on which each group can record what

happens to the characters in their section of the text. The Character Chart could show development in the characters (see Appendix A). The Adventure Chart can be used to show a chronological record of the events which occur in the story. This allows for easy recapitulation of the events in the story and also allows any student who has missed a lesson to catch up on what has happened (see Appendix B).

Caveats and Options

1. An alternative to introducing a text by telling the story is to assign students characters and situations from a text and ask them to create a role-play around the information. Afterwards, explain to them that there is a story about these characters and events and they should start reading it to see how close their ideas were to those of the author.
2. This system can be adapted to all levels according to the text selection. Young beginners particularly enjoy the story telling and role-playing activities. Older students are able to grasp the content of the text without being put off by sophisticated vocabulary.
3. When the students are well into the story, devote a class period to role-playing some of the events.

References and Further Reading

Golding, W. (1958). *The lord of the flies.* London: Faber & Faber.

Collie, J., & Slater, S. (1987). *Literature in the language classroom.* Avon, England: Cambridge University Press.

Appendix A: Sample Character Chart

A Character Chart can be devised to suit student or teacher ideas. It can be augmented as the story progresses. The following is a sample layout.

Chapter	Character	Appearance	Personality	Development	Comments
1	Piggy	fat, glasses	shy, insecure	(for later use)	(this column is for students' opinions)

Appendix B: Sample Adventure Chart

An Adventure Chart can be used for quick reference to what has already occurred in the story and to maintain students' interest as they add events. It may be organized according to student or teacher ideas. The following is a sample layout.

Chapter	What Happened	Result

Contributor

Leanne Wilton works at the English Language Unit, University of Wales Aberystwyth, in the United Kingdom. She has taught ESL in secondary schools and language schools in Turkey and in Australia.

Getting to Know Famous People

Levels
Intermediate

Aims
Read a book
Improve listening
comprehension
Think critically
Teach classmates about
a famous person, using a
grid
Use the library
Write a short
composition or
paragraph

Activity Type
Practice or application

Class Time
1-3 weeks

Preparation Time
1 hour

Resources
Library books

This activity familiarizes students with famous historical figures in an interactive, communicative way. Students teach each other about the famous person each has studied and think about what life would be like if that person had not existed.

Procedure

1. Tell students they will read a biography of a well-known person. You may go to the library first and gather a selection of books and then give students a choice, or take students with you and allow them to choose a biography.
2. Have students read the whole book in class or at home, taking short notes as they read. Encourage them not to use the dictionary for every unknown word, but to read for general understanding. If students are reading in class, circulate as they are reading to answer their questions.
3. Have students answer the questions about their person (see Appendix A). Explain to them that it is necessary for them to understand why that person is important because they will be teaching their biography to at least two other students.
4. After completing Step 3, have students find a partner and complete the grid (see Appendix B). They should exchange information about their biographies by interviewing each other using their charts.
5. After teaching two or more people about the person they researched, students write a short composition about this famous individual. Suggest they organize the composition into three paragraphs on the following topics:

- contributions to society
- what the society was like before the famous person's invention, product, or event
- the effect the person or invention had on others

(See Appendix C for a model.)

If the papers are well done and interesting, tell students you will hang them on a bulletin board in the school, so that other students can learn about famous people.

Caveats and Options

1. Students can decorate a bulletin board in the school with their compositions. They can find a picture of their famous person, copy it, and make a sign to go with their compositions (Print Shop computer software can be used for this purpose). Other students in the school will look at the pictures and read the compositions as they pass by, making it a learning experience for everyone.
2. This activity can be done in a multilevel class. Select books from the library for all reading proficiency levels and distribute to students appropriately. If desired, ask lower level students to write only one or two paragraphs.

References and Further Reading

Huizenga, J., Snellings, C., & Francis, G. (1990). *Basic composition for ESL.* (3rd ed.). Glenview, IL: ScottForesman/Little, Brown.

Price-Machado, D. (1994). An integrated lesson on famous people. *TESOL Journal, 3* (3), 33.

Appendix A: Sample Biography Questions

After you have read your book and taken notes, answer the following questions:

1. What is the name of your famous person?
2. When was that person born? Is that person alive today? If not, when did that person die?
3. What is (or was) your famous person's occupation?
4. What contribution did your person make to our society? When did he or she do the special thing? Write in your own words a few reasons why we think that person is important or famous. Tell how that person affected other people or our history.

5. If your person invented something, what do you think life was like before the invention?

Appendix B: Sample Grid

Work with a partner to fill in the grid. Give each other information orally. Then find one or two more classmates to interview in order to finish the grid.

Student name	Famous person	What the person did and when	Effect on others

Appendix C: Model Composition

Zworykin's contribution to society was developing the technology necessary to make television work. In 1929, Zworykin did research at RCA (Radio Corporation of America) and discovered a device that could change electronic signals into pictures (called a kinescope picture tube). Later, he and his team developed the iconoscope, an electronic tube that changed pictures into electronic signals. Without the iconoscope the TV camera and TV broadcasting would not exist.

Before his inventions, I imagine life was very different. More people got news from newspapers and through word of mouth. Families probably spent more time talking together because they weren't sitting in front of a television set.

Zworykin affected everyone with his inventions, positively and negatively. Because of the TV, we can learn about other countries and get news as it happens. We can learn about animals and even learn a foreign language from television. However, as the article says, average 18-year-olds have spent 20,000 hours watching TV. Unfortunately, many people abuse the television and enjoy it too much instead of doing more constructive things, like reading, exercising, or spending valuable time with their families.

Contributor

Donna Price-Machado has taught all levels of adult ESL for the San Diego Community College District for more than 15 years. She coauthored the District's ESL adult education writing curriculum. She lives and works in California, in the United States.

◆ Developing Language Through Writing Zooming in on Details

Levels
Intermediate

Aims
Learn the importance of detail in writing
Evaluate good instructions
Follow directions

Activity Type
Practice or application

Class Time
1–2 hours, depending upon options chosen

Preparation Time
20–30 minutes

Resources
Colored paper, pencils
Stapler and pair of scissors for each group
Valentine samples made in advance
Copies of both sets of instructions

This activity teaches students why detail in writing is essential for clarity. Also, this activity moves students through the process of evaluating and using details in their writing.

Procedure

1. Before class, prepare a valentine according to the second set of instructions (see Appendix B). Do not show the students the valentine until they have completed their own.
2. Give each group of students the first set of instructions (Appendix A), scissors, a stapler, pencils, and two sheets of colored paper. Ask each group to construct a valentine according to the directions. Resist the urge to help them.
3. After everyone has finished, have the students compare valentines. They will probably be amazed at the variety.
4. Ask them why, if everyone had the exact same instructions, the valentines are so different. They will most likely respond that the directions are too general and inadequate.
5. Repeat the activity using the second set of instructions (Appendix B). Within a few minutes, all the students will have made the same valentine.
6. Have the students evaluate the two sets of instructions by discussing the differences between them. Focus the discussion on the details in the writing.

113

Caveats and Options

1. This activity may be done in groups, in pairs, or individually.
2. Shapes other than a heart may be used. Select easy-to-cut symmetrical shapes, such as a shamrock, pumpkin, Christmas tree, or egg. Be creative!
3. Rather than giving the students the second set of instructions, show them what the valentine should have looked like. Then have students rewrite the instructions. Finally, if possible, have them give the rewritten instructions to a different group of students to see if the instructions are sufficiently clear for this group to make the heart.
4. Build on what the students have learned by having them perform a simple magic trick or demonstrate a science experiment and then critique the result. (Children's books on magic and science projects are excellent sources of simple tricks and experiments.) After the students have performed and demonstrated their tricks or experiments, have the class (as a whole or in groups) evaluate the clarity of the written instructions and rewrite any unclear portions. If the students feel that the instructions were problem-free, they should state what made them good.
5. Ask students to write their own instructions. Students may work in groups or individually. Have the students write instructions for a process (e.g., assembling something, performing a dance step). Have another student or group read and work through the instructions, and afterwards provide feedback to the students who wrote them. The instructions may need to be rewritten several times before there is sufficient detail to accomplish the process adequately.

References and Further Reading

Friedhoffer, R. (1990). *More magic tricks, science facts*. New York: Franklin Watts.

Markle, S. (1988). *Science mini-mysteries: Easy-to-do experiments designed to keep you guessing*. New York: Atheneum.

Severn, B. (1986). *Magic fun for everyone*. New York: E. P. Dutton.

Swezey, K. (1964). *Science shows you how: Exciting experiments that demonstrate basic principles*. New York: McGraw-Hill.

Appendix A: Sample Instructions for a Valentine of Many Hearts, Set 1

Directions: Making a valentine of many hearts is fun, simple, and easy. Fold a piece of red paper. Trace a heart and cut it out. Do it again. Now put all the valentines together to make a valentine flower. Write a note on each one and give it to a friend.

Appendix B: Sample Instructions for a Valentine of Many Hearts, Set 2

Making a valentine of many hearts is fun, simple, and easy.

1. Fold a piece of red paper into fours: Fold it in half from top to bottom, and then fold it in half one more time from left to right.

2. Trace half of a heart onto the side with the fold. With your scissors, cut the heart out. You should have two hearts.

3. Repeat the same process with another piece of paper so that you have four hearts.

4. Now put all four hearts on top of each other, so you cannot see anything but the top one.

5. When you have done that, staple three times along the fold line— once on each outside edge and once in the middle.

   Then open out each valentine half so that it looks like a valentine flower.

   When you are finished, write a nice little note on each of the four individual hearts and give it to a friend.

Contributors

Karen Johnson teaches at Rice University's School of Continuing Studies Language Program, in Texas, in the United States. Her professional interests include materials development and language testing. Jeri Wyn Gillie teaches at Brigham Young University's English Language Center, in Utah, in the United States. Her professional interests include integrated teaching, community building, and materials development.

Holiday Pictures

Levels
Beginning–intermediate

Aims
Practice vocabulary and
sentence writing
Work interdependently

Activity Type
Practice

Class Time
20 minutes

Preparation Time
10 minutes

Resources
3-in. x 5-in. index cards
Copy of a holiday
picture for each team
Long strip of paper for
each team

When students learn together, they can often pick up an idea that they would not see individually. This activity allows students to help each other write longer sentences and include details.

Procedure

1. Group your students into teams of three or four. Make enough teams so that there are 4, 8, or 12 teams.
2. Name the teams: Noun Team, Verb Team, Adjective Team, and Adverb Team.
3. Provide each team with one copy of the same holiday picture.
4. Ask the teams to brainstorm vocabulary. Each team should choose four words connected to their team name that have to do with the holiday in the picture (i.e., nouns if they are the noun team, verbs if they are the verb team). Each person in the team should understand the meaning of the four words.
5. Distribute a 3-in. x 5-in. index card to each student. Each person in the team should copy the four words that the team has chosen on his or her card. (Let the teams check their dictionaries for spelling if necessary.)
6. Separate the team and reassign the students to new teams. Each new team should have a member from the noun, verb, adjective, and adverb teams.
7. Each student brings his or her own card, so the new team will have a collection of 16 words. Make sure each team has one copy of the holiday picture.
8. Ask the students to read their four words to each other and explain the words if necessary.

9. Distribute a long horizontal strip of paper to each team. Each team will write one sentence about the holiday picture using team words. The team with the longest sentence is the winner.

10. The noun person should begin. He or she chooses a noun from the card and writes it as the subject of the sentence on the paper. The paper is passed to the verb person who adds a verb. Next, the adverb person adds an adverb. Last, the adjective person may add an adjective to the subject or ask the noun person to write an object for the sentence. The adjective can then be used with the object.

11. The paper is passed around as long as the team can keep adding to the sentence. When the team members can no longer lengthen the sentence, they raise their hands.

12. Collect all the sentences. Read them to the class. Praise the ideas of each sentence and congratulate the team with the longest one.

Caveats and Options

1. If students do not have an adequate holiday vocabulary base, appropriate words should be introduced in another activity before this activity is used.

2. Use the words to write a short story. Each member of the team should contribute a sentence.

3. Give a small prize to the winning team if appropriate.

4. This activity can be done with other pictures representing a different theme.

Contributor

Wendy Vicens is a lecturer at the American Language and Culture Program at Arizona State University, in the United States. She is active in materials development and computer-assisted language learning.

Author Meets the Artist: Part 1

Levels
Beginning-low
intermediate

Aims
Learn spatial vocabulary
Learn the names of
everyday objects, colors,
patterns, and shapes
Practice brainstorming

Activity Type
Motivation

Class Time
40-50 minutes

Preparation Time
1 hour

Resources
Poster or reproduction
of Vincent Van Gogh's
Bedroom at Arles
Newsprint or overhead
projector and
transparencies
(preferably something
that can be saved)

In this activity, the teacher helps students focus on vocabulary and practice the brainstorming technique of listing to describe a painting.

Procedure

1. Ask students to prepare a piece of paper by writing their name and date in the corner and the word brainstorm on the top line.

2. Introduce Van Gogh's *Bedroom at Arles* very briefly in simple terms. (e.g., "This is a painting. Vincent Van Gogh painted it. He lived in France. Arles is a town in France.")

3. Show a picture of Van Gogh and Arles. Have a student locate Arles on a map.

4. Ask the students to make four columns on their paper. Label the columns: Objects, Colors, Shapes and patterns, Location. (See Appendix for a sample.)

5. Begin the brainstorming activity by pointing to an object in the painting and asking, "What's this?" Call on students who know the answer or allow students to call out the answer. Write the answer in the first column on the newsprint. Direct the students to write the object's name in the first column on their paper.

6. Repeat Step 5 to help students complete the three remaining columns, asking, for example, "What color is it?" "Describe its shape." "Where is it located in the room?"

7. Allow students to supply the needed vocabulary whenever possible. Accept several names for the same item if they are correct. Supply vocabulary where student response is not possible.

8. Review key vocabulary at the end of the period, such as the headings on the paper (e.g., *brainstorm, objects*). Have students define these terms.

Caveats and Options

1. This activity is the first in a series that moves the writer through the steps of the writing process as part of a group.
2. This activity can be used with other paintings, sculptures, or collages. You can access photo files in the Internet to find appropriate art.
3. You can follow up with a spelling test or comprehension test of both the spatial vocabulary and everyday vocabulary.
4. For the most advanced students at this level, try introducing pertinent facts about the artist. Bring in art books or use the Internet files. Students will be fascinated by two of Van Gogh's more spectacular actions: cutting off his ear and committing suicide. Students will be able to use this information later in writing the group essay about the painting.

References and Further Reading

Dishon, D., & Wilson O'Leary, P. (1984). *A guidebook for cooperative learning.* Holmes Beach, FL: Learning Publications.

Elbow, P. (1973). *Writing without teachers.* New York: Oxford University Press.

Freeman, D. E., & Freeman, Y. S. (1992). *Whole language for second language learners*. Portsmouth, NH: Heinemann Press.

Raimes, A. (1983). *Techniques in teaching writing*. New York: Oxford University Press.

Appendix: Sample Chart

Brainstorm			
Objects	*Colors*	*Shapes and Patterns*	*Location*
a chair	brown		on the north wall between the bed and the table
window	yellow green	rectangles	on the north wall between the mirror and the picture
a blanket	red	plain	on the bed
two pillows	yellow	rectangles	at the head of the bed
a towel	light yellow		next to the door on the east wall hanging from a hook

Contributor

Lyn Froning has taught ESL at the middle and high school levels for 25 years in American Samoa and in Maryland, Hawaii, Massachusetts, and Alabama, in the United States.

Author Meets the Artist: Part 2

Levels
Beginning–low
intermediate

Aims
Review vocabulary for
everyday objects, colors,
patterns, and shapes
Practice organization
Recognize categories

Activity Type
Motivation

Class Time
40-50 minutes

Preparation Time
30 minutes

Resources
Poster or reproduction
of Vincent Van Gogh's
Bedroom at Arles
Brainstorm list of
objects, colors, shapes
and patterns, and spatial
vocabulary describing
the painting from
"Author Meets the Artist:
Part 1"
Two to three pictures of
food from the food
groups (dairy, grains,
fruits, vegetables, meat)

Students continue their prewriting activity from Part 1, working in pairs or triads to organize the objects on their brainstorming sheet.

Procedure

1. Show the students the food pictures and ask them to name the items. Write these names on the blackboard in a list entitled, Brainstorm.
2. Next to the brainstorming list, draw a semantic map (see Appendix). Use this map to categorize the names of the food. Leave the center circle blank.
3. Ask students to organize the foods listed in Step 1 by categories and place names in the circles that surround the center circle. Usually students see readily which foods go together.
4. After the names are distributed to the appropriate circles, ask the students to label each circle (e.g., by food group). Write these labels over the top of each circle.
5. Ask the students to label the entire chart with one or two words. Write this label in the center circle. This label is the title for the semantic map.
6. Divide the students into pairs or triads and explain that the next activity will use the objects from the brainstorm list they made about Van Gogh's "Bedroom at Arles" (see "Author Meets The Artist: Part 1").
7. Give each pair or triad one piece of paper and one pen. The paper may be a copy of the map used in Step 2, or a student may draw the outline of the map on the paper. Assign roles. One person will draw the map and write in the names of the objects and the partner(s) will dictate what to write. Students may switch roles every 10 minutes.
8. Instruct each pair or triad to complete the map using the names of the bedroom objects from their brainstorms about Van Gogh's

picture. The students should work together to categorize the objects. They need not write the colors, shapes, patterns, or spatial vocabulary at this time, but they will use this information later. After they complete the categorization, instruct the students to label each circle and finally label the circle in the middle.

9. Ask groups to share their maps after they have finished and signed their names to them.

Caveats and Options

1. This exercise is the second in a series that takes the writer through the steps of the writing process as part of a group.
2. If a student, pair, or triad has difficulty with any of the steps, encourage them to complete as much as they can. Help them by referring them to the food model. Each pair or group may see the organization differently; therefore it is important not to impose one idea as the correct one. During the sharing time, they can gain further insight into the organization process by seeing the different ways students have chosen to fill out their maps.
3. Planning how the students will be paired or grouped works best. Do not let the students choose their partners. Mix languages whenever possible. For this exercise, what works well is to group two students at the same level with one lower level student. To start, the lower level student may be the recorder.
4. The teacher should monitor the group work closely by helping students with process as well as content. Make sure students stick to their roles as the one who records or the one who dictates. Each role is important and allows the students to practice different skills. Maintaining the roles also ensures that each student will participate. The one who dictates should not hold the pen; it is sometimes necessary for the teacher to make sure this does not happen.

References and Further Reading

Dishon, D., & Wilson O'Leary, P. (1984). *A guidebook for cooperative learning.* Holmes Beach, FL: Learning Publications.

Elbow, P. (1973). *Writing without teachers.* New York: Oxford University Press.

Freeman, D.E., & Freeman, Y.S. (1992). *Whole language for second language learners*. Portsmouth, NH: Heinemann.

Raimes, A. (1983). *Techniques in teaching writing*. New York: Oxford University Press.

Appendix: Sample Semantic Map

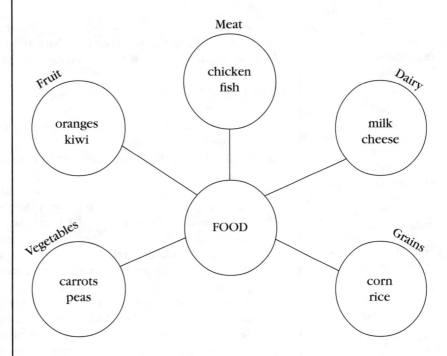

Contributor

Lyn Froning has taught ESL at the middle and high school levels for 25 years in American Samoa and in Maryland, Hawaii, Massachusetts, and Alabama, in the United States.

Author Meets the Artist: Part 3

Levels
Beginning–low
intermediate

Aims
Review spatial
vocabulary and names of
everyday objects, colors,
patterns, and shapes
Practice use of
expressions *there is…,*
there are…
Practice drafting
Write short paragraphs

Activity Type
Motivation or practice

Class Time
One or two 40- to 50-
minute periods

Preparation Time
30 minutes

Resources
Poster or reproduction of
Vincent Van Gogh's
Bedroom at Arles
Brainstorm list from
Part 1
Semantic maps from
Part 2
Overhead projector and
transparencies

Students continue the prewriting activity from Parts 1 and 2 of this activity to create a rough draft of an essay on Van Gogh's painting.

Procedure

1. Before class, draw or type each group's semantic map onto an overhead transparency.
2. Begin class by displaying one group's map on the overhead projector.
3. Instruct the students to have their own written brainstorms from "Author Meets the Artist, Part 1" (pp. 118–120) ready to add colors, shapes and patterns, and spatial vocabulary to the sentences that they, with the teacher, are now going to write.
4. Point to the middle circle on the map on the overhead. Elicit from the students information they remember about Van Gogh and or the painting.
5. As the students provide this information, write it in complete sentence form on the blackboard or newsprint. Indent the first sentence so that this information will form the first paragraph. The topic sentence and sentence order within the paragraph are best dealt with at a later stage in the students' writing. However, sentences can be rearranged to make better sense during the editing stage as necessary.
6. Preteach or incorporate the use of the expressions *there is* and *there are* because they are commonly used with spatial vocabulary.
7. Have the students suggest which circle on the semantic map to use for the next paragraph. Then elicit the information about the objects in that circle: the names, colors, and place of each one, including shape and pattern if appropriate. Write the sentences exactly as the

students say them. If an error is detected by another student, you may want to stop to discuss it and correct it.

8.   Continue to elicit each circle's information from the students. Begin a new paragraph with each circle.

9.   When that group's composition is complete, project another group's map on the screen and begin again. It is not necessary to write a composition for each group's map, but complete as many as are necessary for the class to internalize the procedures.

10.   The three-part lesson unit ends here. Teachers may continue to work with students on editing their paragraphs and creating final copy. Or, they may move on to related writing topics (see options) and repeat this three-step process.

Caveats and Options

1.   Using newsprint is preferable because the compositions can be hung around the room as reminders and models when the students are writing solo about their own bedrooms.

2.   Do not correct spelling or grammar errors unless attention is called to them by students themselves. However, do not make an incorrect change at the direction of the students. Most errors will be dealt with during an editing step. However, at this proficiency level, it is not necessary or expected for students to write perfect sentences.

3.   Emphasize that a rough draft is not a perfect copy. Demonstrate this by crossing out errors and writing the corrections above or next to the crossed out words.

4.   As an alternative to this activity, students can work in triads using their own map to write the rough draft. Apply the rules from caveat two above. If the writer is constantly whiting out or starting over on clean paper to avoid making mistakes, emphasize that crossing out changes and writing new thoughts above or next to the crossed out words saves time and paper. The teacher should monitor this process by walking around the room observing and advising each group as they work. Students can share and edit rough drafts as a next step.

5.   Students can draw sketches of their own bedrooms and then use the brainstorm, mapping, and drafting process to write stories about them.

6. A variation would be for pairs of students to interview each other about the location of objects in each other's bedrooms. Only the interviewer is allowed to use a pencil. The interviewee must describe his or her own bedroom verbally, after which the interviewer draws a picture of it.

7. Students can use the brainstorm, mapping, and drafting steps to write their idea of a perfect bedroom. Editing and final copies can follow.

References and Further Reading

Dishon, D., & Wilson O'Leary, P. (1984). *A guidebook for cooperative learning.* Holmes Beach, FL: Learning Publications.

Elbow, P. (1973). *Writing without teachers.* New York: Oxford University Press.

Freeman, D.E., & Freeman, Y.S. (1992). *Whole language for second language learners.* Portsmouth, NH: Heinemann.

Raimes, A. (1983). *Techniques in teaching writing.* New York: Oxford University Press.

Contributor

Lyn Froning has taught ESL at the middle and high school levels for 25 years in American Samoa and in Maryland, Hawaii, Massachusetts, and Alabama, in the United States.

Crystal Ball Writings

Levels
High beginning–
intermediate; high
school

Aims
Reflect on the direction
of their lives
Write paragraphs
Improve vocabulary and
sentence structure
Practice listening
comprehension

Activity Type
Application

Class Time
2 hours

Preparation Time
30 minutes

Resources
Paper and pencil

S tudents reflect on their past, present, and future, then write a paragraph about these times in their lives. Classmates choose unidentified paragraphs to read aloud and the class tries to guess who wrote the paragraph.

Procedure

1. Have students write three paragraphs, one each about
   - their past: childhood or youth, family and friends, their country
   - their present: school, family, work, favorite activities, hobbies, interests, friends
   - their future: what they want for their future (e.g., marriage, family, career), where they will live
2. Ask students to edit and copy each paragraph onto a separate piece of paper.
3. Tell the students to fold each paragraph into a small square.
4. Put all of the paragraphs into a box or other container.
5. Call on a student to select a paragraph from the box and read it aloud to the class. A past, present, or future paragraph might be drawn.
6. Class members try to guess who wrote the paragraph and give reasons for their guesses.
7. The student who guesses the author correctly selects and reads the next paragraph to the class.

Caveats and Options

1. The teacher should remind students not to write anything very personal that they would not want to share with the whole class.
2. If students have not done much writing, review basic writing procedures, such as: drafting, organizing, topic sentences followed by

details, and editing for grammar, usage, capitalization, and punctuation.

3. Students may require more than the allotted time to complete this activity.

Contributor

Marlene M. Ryder (BA and MEd in languages and teaching), teaches high school ESL in Virginia, in the United States and has taught French and Spanish at university and secondary levels.

The Personality Exploration Exercise

Levels
Intermediate +

Aims
Create a personality
profile
Use persuasive speech
Enjoy using English
Practice writing

Activity Type
Motivation

Class Time
1 hour

Preparation Time
2 hours

Resources
Personality profile
handouts

The profiles offer students adjective-packed descriptions of their person-alities that include both strengths and weaknesses. Although they are not necessarily accurate descriptions, each of the descriptions allows the students a starting point to describe who they are.

Procedure

1. Write personality profiles for your class using many new adjectives. Try to write one profile for each student in the class based on what you observe from your interactions with them. The paragraphs could include strengths and weaknesses of the individuals. These para-graphs should motivate students to construct an argument describing who they are. Below are some examples:
    *   You are impulsive, emotional, impatient, and like to get results quickly. You have originality and good judgment and are versatile and quick to grasp a point. You have a keen sense of humor, are winsome and vivacious, loving, and demonstrative in your family. You make your home pleasant and attractive.
    *   You are a private person and do not like to be questioned about your own affairs or the affairs of anyone else. You are ambitious and resourceful, impulsive and emotional, and are guided by your intuition. You love your home and family and are capable of a deep and fervent love.
2. Compile all profiles onto one handout and make copies for each student. After giving each student the prepared profiles handout, ask students to select the description that comes closest to their character.
3. For homework or as a classroom activity, have students write an essay persuading the reader that the personality they chose suits them best. Share these with the class, if desired.

4. Identify for the students the description you intended for each one of them.
5. This can be followed up with a rebuttal. Ask students to write a response paper to the description that corresponds to what you wrote about them.
6. Allow students to select new adjectives to describe themselves from the list of profiles to add to their vocabulary base. This activity should help to build rapport between the instructor and students.

Caveats and Options

1. This activity can be adapted as a spoken exercise if the number of students is limited. It can be an interview as well, in which you require students to learn to use new adjectives to promote themselves.
2. This activity can be adapted for beginners by changing the choice of adjectives and length of the profiles.
3. Students can work in pairs to discuss their personalities or to get some feedback on the perception others have of them.
4. Students can write entries for themselves or for their classmates. The class can compile these profiles to make an original personality book.

References and Further Reading

Tani-Hayes, N. (1994). The birthday book. *TESOL Journal 4* (1), 50–51.

Contributor

Naoko Tani has a BA from Wellesley College, and an MA in TESOL and an MEd in counseling psychology from Teachers College, Columbia University. She currently teaches at Kwansei Gakuin University in Japan.

Who Stole Mari's Wallet?

Levels
Intermediate; high
school

Aims
Write about an event
Scan for information

Activity Type
Motivation

Class Time
2 hours for 3 days

Preparation Time
1 hour for 2 days

Resources
Student-produced
compositions
Question list for each
student

S tudents write better when they know their work will be read, and they read better when they are interested. This writing-reading activity generates real effort and concentration because students like to share their experiences and are interested in one another.

Procedure

1. Day 1: Assign each student a short composition on the topic of an important personal experience, such as the student's most embarrassing, frightening, or exciting moment. A good topic is a crime witnessed, heard about, or experienced by the writer or someone close. Collect and review. Write editing suggestions on each of the papers.

2. Day 2: Return the compositions for revision with your suggestions for improvement and tell the writers that their revised papers will be shared with all their classmates. Collect the revisions, but do not edit or mark them. In preparation for Day 3, prepare a list of questions on a separate sheet of paper, choosing one interesting detail from each composition and identifying the writer. Select details that are small enough to require close reading and near the endings, if possible.

3. Day 3: Distribute the list of questions to the class explaining that they cannot ask for the answers but must read for them. Return the revised compositions to their authors and let them fasten their papers to the walls around the room, making sure they are at eye level and spaced out so that they can be read easily without crowding. Instruct the students to walk around the room, reading for the answers. When everyone has answered all the questions on the list and turned in their papers, the students enjoy discussing their experiences.

Caveats and Options

1. Either the first draft or the revision, or both, can be done outside of class.
2. Writers can contribute their own three questions about their compositions, from which the teacher will choose one.

Contributor

Janet Caglan is a lecturer in the College of Extended Education at Arizona State University, in the United States.

The Monday Letter: A New Twist on Journal Writing

Levels
Any

Aims
Read and interpret
information in a letter
format
Practice letter-writing
techniques
Construct weekly letters

Activity Type
Motivation

Class Time
30 minutes

Preparation Time
20 minutes

Resources
Overhead transparencies
and projector

The Monday Letter, written by the teacher about the previous weekend's activities and thoughts, sparks students' reading, writing and vocabulary skills as they interpret the contents of the letter. It serves as a catalyst for students to write their own Monday Letters describing their weekend activities or things they are thinking about.

Procedure

1. On Sunday evening, write a one-page letter to your class describing some of the things that you did over the weekend. Try to organize the weekend into key topics; each topic may have its own paragraph. That way, students see how a topic sentence introduces each paragraph and that each paragraph has key vocabulary related to the topic. (See Sample Letter 1 in Appendix A.)
2. Make an overhead transparency of the Monday Letter.
3. On Monday, read the letter aloud as a class and discuss. As appropriate, point out the organization, paragraph structure, use of descriptive vocabulary, "writer's voice," expressions used to convey thoughts and feelings, and more.
4. Have students respond to your letter by writing their own Monday Letter every Monday evening for homework. At first, the student responses may seem simple and resemble a laundry list of basic activities like getting up, taking a shower, watching television, and so forth. However, after exposure to reading the teacher's letters, and seeing the role of descriptive vocabulary and varied language structures, the students should start to include more details about their weekend activities. They may also start to organize their letters around a central theme and try to include vocabulary and structures that they are learning in class. (See student samples in Appendix B.)

5. In class on Tuesday, you may ask students to volunteer to read their letters aloud before collecting them.
6. Write a response to each student letter as you would do for a journal entry.
7. Keep sample letters for each student from the beginning, middle, and end of the school year to compare student writing and language growth.

Caveats and Options

1. I recommend typing the letter on the computer because this makes it easy for the class to read. I generally use an 18-point font so the students can see it easily, too.
2. For a change, duplicate the Monday Letter and distribute it to all the students so they can read it independently.
3. After students read the teacher's Monday Letter either on the overhead or as a paper copy, they can take a listening comprehension quiz on the contents of the letter. (See sample based on Letter 1 in Appendix C.) This is a great way for students to review vocabulary, grammar, and other language structures. Quite often, I might introduce a language construction, such as the present perfect tense, in my Monday Letter so students might have exposure to it before they meet it within their text.
4. As another option, instead of writing a complete letter, use the cloze format and ask students to insert a word that would make sense. Because some commercial reading tests use this method (e.g., Degrees of Reading Power), it is good practice for the students. You can also assess students' ability to construct meaning if they could insert an appropriate word in the sentence. Afterward, the class can talk about word choice, synonyms, and so on. (See sample in Appendix D.)
5. You may want to vary the students' assignment. Instead of always writing about their weekend, you may ask them to share personal goals, hopes, and concerns.
6. Over time, students start incorporating reading strategies such as identifying the main idea, understanding vocabulary in context, and summarizing, as they begin to read the letters more critically.

7. Clear writing and organization are important criteria for our state writing test, and the Monday Letter becomes a model for these criteria. At the beginning of the year, the students and I talk about how I organized the letter and why I have different paragraphs for different topics and how I introduce each paragraph.

8. One beneficial outcome of the Monday Letter has been to give students more information about cultural events and topics beyond the textbook. Once I wrote about my son's high school Homecoming football game and dance and described the formal gowns and tuxedos that the students wore. My students will participate in homecoming activities and need to know about some of these topics.

Appendix A: Monday Letter, Sample 1

November

Dear HILT [High Intensity Language Training] B Class,

Are your families as busy as mine preparing for Thanksgiving? The supermarket was so crowded this past weekend with everyone buying turkeys, squash, sweet potatoes, and pumpkin pies. The only good thing about all this work is that families have an opportunity to celebrate being together again. Some day you will be in charge of planning your own Thanksgiving dinner!

Everyone commended you on your performance last Friday. The teachers said that you acted maturely and were very organized and prepared for your roles. Now the other students want to do a play like ours. You should be proud that you were such good role models.

On Sunday my husband and I took Misty on a long walk in the parkland not far from our house. We took off her leash so she could run freely. The only problem was that Misty is a yellow Labrador retriever and Labrador dogs love water. There is a creek that runs through the park, and naturally, Misty jumped in about five different times. I was upset because the creek water was filthy and I had to hose her down when we got home. The only good thing is I know she won't drown because she's a natural-born swimmer.

I hope you all have a wonderful Thanksgiving with your families.

Sincerely,
Mrs. Fagan

**Appendix B:
Sample
Student
Monday
Letters**

9-14-92

Dear Mrs. Fagan

When I whent To played soccer.
I played with my father's friends.
and when I was playing with then.
they pushed me many times because
they're To big.

When I was playing football with
my friends I was happy becouse
I like to play football.

May 8, 1995

Dear Mrs. Fagan,

I had an exciting weekend. I have done two things, go to the moll and go to a picknick with my family.

On Saturday I went to the mall to try to find a bell for mrs. Melnick's sorprised but I couln't find it, so I decided to buy another thing, I bought a notbook where you can write address or telephones from people and other things too. I can wate mrs. Melnick's face when she sees the sorpresen we have for her.

On Sunday was a great day. My family and I when to a park that is almost from my house. Where you can cook outdoors, rite your bike or plays ball and you also can catch fish from the lake.

Sencerely.

Appendix C: Listening Comprehension Questions for Monday Letter, Sample 1

1. What is the main idea of Paragraph 1?
2. Name three popular Thanksgiving foods.
3. What is the benefit of this holiday?
4. What is the main idea of Paragraph 2?
5. Find a word in Paragraph 2 that means "a play."
6. Find a word in Paragraph 2 that means "someone to admire."
7. Find a word in Paragraph 2 that means "you did a good job."
8. What is the main idea of Paragraph 3?
9. What breed of dog is Misty?
10. Find a word in Paragraph 3 that means "a small river."

BONUS: Find a word in Paragraph 3 that means "the opposite of clean."

Appendix D: Monday Letter, Sample Cloze Version

January

Dear Class,

Welcome back to a new year and just __1__ more years to a new millennium! Did any of you do something special to celebrate the beginning of 1998? Some people have New Year's Eve __2__ where people wear funny __3__ on their heads and blow horns and drink champagne at __4__. I had a quiet New Year's Eve with my family and then on New Year's Day, we had an Open House for our neighbors. What do you think an Open House is?

The New Year is a time for reflection and __5__ about making our lives better. People like to make New Year's Resolutions which help them __6__ things that they haven't done before. One of my __7__ is to get more physical exercise to keep my body __8__. What were some of your resolutions?

In two weeks we will be having another _____9_____ in our class. She will be working with me and I think you will like having two teachers work together.

Let's try to make this a great New Year!

Sincerely,

Mrs. Fagan

Contributor

Barbara Fagan is the ESOL/HILT (High Intensity Language Training) Secondary Specialist and a middle school teacher for Arlington Public Schools in Virginia, in the United States.

Drawing Lessons

Levels
Beginning-intermediate;
middle school

Aims
Use drawings as a
resource for developing
language skills
Practice writing and
speaking

Activity Type
Application

Class Time
20 minutes +

Preparation Time
30 minutes +

Resources
Reading selections
related to the topic of
the lesson
Paper and crayons

This approach incorporates students' artwork/drawings with language learning activities that may involve a single language skill, such as writing, or additional language skills, such as reading and speaking.

Procedure

1. Discuss with students an event, such as an earthquake, flood, or major fire, that most of them may have experienced. Have students work independently to draw what the event looked like on white paper, leaving a quarter of the space for writing.
2. Next, have students read and discuss texts related to the lesson topic. For example, if the topic is Earthquakes, students will read and discuss texts on earthquakes and learn useful words for their writing. Highlight the key terms (e.g., *earthquake, aftershock, epicenter, helicopter, ambulance, freeway, damage, gas main,* and *electricity*), and ask students to copy expressions that may come in handy when they write a description of their pictures later.
3. Have students write about their own pictures and revise their writing through guided group work. Students
   - write a draft of the picture description on a separate piece of paper, using words learned from reading
   - exchange drafts with a partner and check one another's spelling, capitalization, and punctuation
   - turn in the drafts to the teacher, who underlines parts that need clarification and improvement (but ignores minor errors)
   - revise the text in groups, with feedback from peers
   - get teacher approval of the revised drafts
   - write the final version of the text in the space reserved on the paper with the drawing (see Appendix for a student work sample of "Earthquake")

4. Prepare students for oral presentations so they can talk about their pictures in class and answer questions. Explain that they will talk for 3 minutes and then respond to questions from their peers. If needed, review the types of questions the students might ask one another about the drawings.

5. Facilitate the oral presentations. This could be the most exciting part of the lesson because students have a good opportunity to interact with peers and to evaluate each other's work. Students may make their presentations more effective through role-playing, mime, and sound to reflect the sensations of the experience.

Caveats and Options

1. Language teaching can be more motivating and effective when it is combined with learners' interests and needs. ESL students often feel frustrated when they have more emotions than words in English to express them. However, they may express their feelings and experiences more easily by drawing pictures. I do drawing lessons about once a month. For each session, the students spend about 20 minutes for simple drawing and writing, or longer periods for more careful work. I begin with guided exercises: Students draw pictures to illustrate descriptions from a textbook; students draw pictures and write their own descriptions; students look at a picture and write freely about it. Then we do drawings as described in this activity.

2. If your class has not experienced an "event," another option is to have students draw their vision for the future; readings could relate to futuristic ideas or forecasts of the future.

3. A teacher does not have to be able to draw in order to conduct this activity, but does need to know how to make use of drawing and incorporate it with subject matter. (I myself cannot draw, and students take care of their own artistic endeavors.)

4. This is a very flexible activity which can be a simple "drawing and writing" exercise or be expanded to a project with a topic that may involve the practice of all language skills, such as, "My Culture," "Our Community," or "Save the Endangered Animals."

5. Students' work is the best decoration for the classroom. It will not only encourage academic achievements but also beautify the learning environment in a meaningful and economical way.

Appendix: Sample Student Artwork

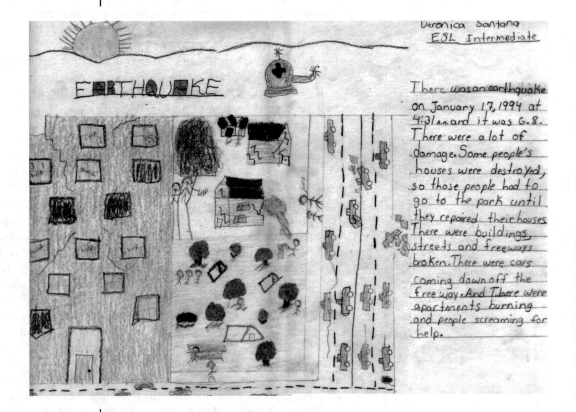

Acknowledgment

Special thanks to my former teacher, Lise Winer, for her valuable comments and suggestions.

Contributor

Yue Huang teaches ESL at George Washington Carver Middle School, in California, in the United States.

Picture Writing

Levels
Intermediate +

Aims
Practice creative writing skills
Assess individual student writing levels

Activity Type
Practice or assessment

Class Time
50 minutes

Preparation Time
1–2 hours (the first time)

Resources
Magazines, scissors, construction paper, glue (optional)

This activity can used as a class writing activity or as an assessment of individual writing skills. It can be repeated multiple times to show writing skills development.

Procedure

1. Review the writing process with students, reminding them of the prewriting activities you may have worked on before: brainstorming, organizing or categorizing (semantic mapping), story mapping, character development, identification of a problem and its solution (plot planning), and so forth.
2. Cut out pictures from magazines (e.g., women's, sports, and news magazines) in the following categories: people, places, things, and activities. You may mount them on construction paper if desired. You will need two or three pictures per category per student, except in the people category, for which you will need four to six.
3. Place the pictures by categories on tables around the room. Label with stand-up signs: People, Places, Things, Activities. Let students go to the tables (two at a time per table) and select one picture from each category except the "People" category, from which they should select two.
4. Have students write a story based on the five pictures they have selected. The story should be at least two pages long. Encourage them to use preliminary parts of the writing process, such as brainstorming or outlining, before they start writing.
5. Use this writing piece as a tool to help students improve a particular aspect of writing, determined by your objectives and individual student needs. For example, if students need help with capital letters, review the capitalization rules and let students proofread their stories

for capitalization and make corrections. If you are studying subject-verb agreement, ask students to locate the subjects and determine if they are singular or plural and then check the verbs to see whether they are in agreement.

6. Ask students to return the pictures to the tables when they are finished. The stories can become part of a student's portfolio, to show writing development. Students can edit and revise any of these pieces for future writing assignments.

Caveats and Options

1. Before doing this on an individual basis, do it together as a class, projecting pictures on the overhead, or by using large pictures that can be seen by all students at once. Write a class story together to practice the procedure.
2. This activity can be repeated indefinitely by adding new pictures to the selections.
3. Students can select pictures from magazines for other students to write about.

References and Further Reading

Calkins, L. M. (1986). *The art of teaching writing*. Portsmouth, NH: Heinemann.

Contributor

Joan M. Dungey has taught ESL at all levels and is an author of numerous journal articles and a frequent presenter at TESOL conferences.

Comic Strips

Levels
Beginning; middle
school

Aims
Revise and extend
vocabulary
Revise and extend use
of tenses
Develop awareness of
text structure
Practice storytelling

Activity Type
Review or application

Class Time
1 hour +

Preparation Time
1 hour

Resources
Comic strips

This activity can be used to revise or introduce language structures, vocabulary, and simple narrative patterns, including the use of dialogue in a text. The use of direct and indirect speech can also be explored.

Procedure

1. Choose some popular cartoon strips (of about four panels in length), blank out the words, and cut the sequence of pictures (panels) apart.
2. Give the cartoons to the students and ask them to work in teams of two or four to put the pictures into the correct order. Explain that they need to be prepared to explain why they have chosen this order and to narrate an original comic strip story.
3. Walk around the class and help students with any vocabulary they need. Check that they are being consistent with the tense they are using to tell the story.
4. When teams have finished, ask them to form larger groups of approximately six to eight students. Ask each team to tell the story and explain the order it chose to others in the group.
5. Students should choose one story from their group to relate to the class. One member of the group should tell the story.
6. Encourage the other groups to ask questions about the events, dialogue, and characters in the story.
7. Elicit from each group information about the structure of the story, such as the order of events, an introduction to the comic situation, a conclusion, and so forth. Have the group come to consensus and give reasons for the choice.

8. Ask students to write their own story based on their original comic strip and encourage them to think about the questions that they have been asked.
9. Remind students that they can rewrite the story several times and that this is their first draft.
10. Walk around and help students with the structure of the story and the addition of new information.
11. Ask students to write a final draft.

Caveats and Options

1. With short cartoons that use only sound words, introduce the use of sound words to the students.
2. All students can work on the same cartoons, or you can assign different ones to different teams. For longer comic strips, the story can be divided between teams around the class. When the teams work in the larger group, they will have to pool information to agree on the order of the comic strip pictures.
3. The writing can be done as pair work or a group activity.
4. Stories can be used as wall displays or shared with other classes.

Contributor

Jackie Wheeler works as a lecturer for the Hong Kong Institute of Education, training teachers and teaching ESL. She has worked at the tertiary and secondary levels.

Write-Up

Levels
Beginning–intermediate;
middle school

Aims
Write in English

Activity Type
Motivation

Class Time
1 hour

Preparation Time
10 minutes

Resources
Popular teen magazine
containing pictures of
pop idols
Large sheets of paper
Sticky tape

This activity uses the pupils' knowledge about popular entertainers from music and films to motivate them to write in English.

Procedure

1. Select a number of pictures of pop idols from the teen magazine.
2. Make posters by sticking a picture of an idol in the middle of each large sheet of paper. Make sure there is a lot of free space around the picture.
3. Put the posters on the walls around the classroom.
4. Ask the pupils to walk around the classroom and write anything they know about the persons pictured directly on the posters, in English.
5. Tell the pupils not to talk to each other.
6. Stop the pupils when enough information has been written on each poster.
7. Form groups and assign a group to each poster. You might ask students to form groups according to their favorite idol.
8. Tell the groups to work collaboratively to correct any errors in the comments written on their posters.
9. Circulate and help the students with both spelling and ideas as needed.
10. Then ask each student to use the information from his or her group's poster to write a short piece about the idol. Possible topics might include personal history, most famous songs or movies, or physical description.
11. Collect the student work and assess it.

Caveats and Options

1. The students could circulate their written pieces within their groups and peer-correct.
2. You may wish to display a model of the kind of writing required.
3. Step 10 may be done as a group- or pair-writing task if the students have difficulty doing it by themselves.

Contributors

Lindsay Miller is an assistant professor in the English Department at City University of Hong Kong. David Gardner is a senior language instructor in the English Centre of The University of Hong Kong.

Stories-Go-Round

Levels
Beginning–intermediate

Aims
Be creative and
expressive in writing
Review vocabulary
Practice reading

Activity Type
Application or review

Class Time
30 minutes

Preparation Time
30 minutes

Resources
Story-starting sentences
written on index cards

This activity stimulates students' creativity as they generate cooperative stories while passing around their papers. The final products of this activity are complete stories for each student.

Procedure

1. Arrange students in groups of six to eight. Number the groups and have them sit in a circle. Explain to them that they will create stories by passing their papers around the circle.
2. Distribute one story starter card per student (see Appendix) and direct the students to write their name and group number on a sheet of lined composition paper. Ask the students to copy the story starter on the paper and add one sentence of their own to continue the story.
3. Ask students to pass their paper to the person to their left. Tell them to read the story as written so far and add another sentence.
4. As the students continue to pass the story along, with each adding a sentence, circulate to assist as needed.
5. After 15–20 minutes, ask the group leaders to call on students to read stories aloud in their groups. If time is available, ask each group to choose one story to read to the whole class.

Caveats and Options

1. You may want to assign students to work in pairs on revision and correction.
2. For homework or during the next class, you may want to have each student prepare a final version of the group's story.
3. After students have tried your story starters, you might want to have them create their own. These story starters can be based on a genre,

149

like a fable or newspaper article, or on a certain theme or topic, perhaps connected to something else they are studying.

4. This activity works well when tied into a grammar point you want students to practice. For example, all the stories could start with the past tense (*When I was in Italy, I saw . . .*) or they could use superlatives (*David, one of the most generous people I have ever known, . . .*).

5. You may also want to ask students to illustrate their stories.

References and Further Reading

Zelman, N.E. (1986). *Conversation inspirations for ESL*. Brattleboro, VT: Pro Lingua Associates.

Appendix: Sample Story Starters

One day a large van filled with thousands of balloons was driving down the highway.

One day an enormous noise was heard in the house.

One day a large family decided to take a walk on a deserted beach.

* * *

As John was walking down the street, he heard a loud roar.

As Mary was hiking up the mountain, she saw a huge animal.

As the farmer was working in his garden, he spied a tremendous rock.

* * *

Last week I took a trip to a space station.

Ten years ago I was a confused student.

Last night I had a horrible dream.

* * *

Nancy's mother was shocked when she heard her daughter say, "Yes, John, I'll go with you."

Pierre couldn't believe his ears! His father said, "Well, son, here are the keys. They're yours."

Just as Salina was about to run, she heard José shout, "Stay put!"

Contributor

Maxine Endy teaches at Clara Barton High School for Health Professions. She has presented on literacy and content-based instruction at TESOL conventions and for the New York City Board of Education.

Poster Adaptations of Short Stories

Levels
Intermediate +; high school

Aims
Practice writing paragraphs
Learn how to summarize information
Build vocabulary and improve sentence structure

Activity Type
Application or review

Class Time
50 minutes

Preparation Time
15-30 minutes

Resources
Lined poster board
Colored markers

Students write a lively summary of part of a short story, copy it onto poster board with markers, and colorfully illustrate it. Then group members present their posters to the class as a complete short story.

Procedure

1. Announce to students that they will be conducting the class.
2. Discuss a short story they read the previous day (or recently) to refresh memories.
3. Divide the class into groups of three or four students.
4. Assign a separate section of the short story to each group. Groups do the following:
   - write a summary paragraph (7-9 sentences) of the assigned section
   - have the teacher review the paragraph for correct grammar, usage, and punctuation
   - copy the paragraph onto the poster board, leaving enough space for illustrations
   - illustrate the paragraph or an aspect of it on the poster using the colored markers
   - tape posters to the blackboard or wall following the sequence of the story
5. Have a student from each group read that group's poster to the class. Continue reading all posters, following the sequence of the story. Repeat the process with different students, as time permits.

Caveats and Options

1. Students can draw the illustrations first, then copy the paragraph onto the poster.
2. This activity could also be done with chapters in a book.
3. Be sure to select stories that can be easily divided into sections. I used this activity with two stories, "The Poor Woman's Gift" (Mundahl, 1993) and "A White Heron" (Jewett, 1988).
4. Assign one good artist to each group, if possible.

References and Further Reading

Jewett, S.O. (1988). A white heron. In B. Goodman (Ed.), *Spotlight on literature collection 2* (pp. 60–65). New York: McGraw Hill.

Mundahl, J. (1993). The poor woman's gift. In *Tales of courage, tales of dreams* (pp. 52–57). Reading, MA: Addison-Wesley.

Contributor

Marlene M. Ryder (BA and MEd in languages and teaching) teaches high school ESL in Virginia, in the United States, and has taught French and Spanish at university and secondary levels.

Part III: Connections With Content Areas

Editor's Note

The two sets of activities in this section examine the ways content can be integrated with language learning, a critical aspect in the secondary school education of English language learners. In the first set, "Integrating Language with Academic Content," general activities that can apply to multiple content areas and texts are presented along with activities designed with a specific subject area in mind: social studies, science, health, and math. The range of tasks for students includes the integration of all language skills. Several contributions add art, drama, and field trips to the language- and content-learning process.

"Survival and Career Orientation," the second set of activities, allows teachers to focus on students' lives beyond school. Some of these activities help students practice survival skills such as reading maps, getting a job, and finding a home. Other activities enable students to learn about expectations, experiences, and credentials needed for careers, including the academic preparation required for certain occupations and the college entrance process, which may be different in the students' home countries.

◆ Integrating Language With Academic Content

Access Content With Graphic Organizers

Levels
Beginning–intermediate

Aims
Connect key concepts
Learn key vocabulary

Activity Type
Motivation or review

Class Time
10–20 minutes

Preparation Time
30–60 minutes

Resources
Text and other
information sources
Overhead projector and
transparencies
Blackboard

This activity may be used as an introduction or a review to create a visual connection between key concepts and vocabulary in the context of an experience, a simulation, an experiment, a demonstration, or a discussion.

Procedure

1. Examine content material to be learned to determine the key concepts and their relationships to each other. Decide which type of graphic organizer suits the content and the relationships of the key concepts. In this example, there is one main concept, three subordinate concepts, and a number of examples of each.

2. Connect the new content with students' prior understandings through an experience, demonstration, simulation, discussion, or other means. If the activity is used to introduce new material or to motivate students, the students' prior understandings would be primarily their own background experience, although the organizer could be coordinated with a demonstration or simulation. If the activity is used for review, it would draw upon the reading, discussion, and other activities that formed the lesson. In this particular example, students could examine various geometric figures in text illustrations, on the chalkboard, overhead transparencies, the computer, or by using geometric models.

3. As the students experience and discuss the content, provide a graphic skeleton and a list of key terms that will go on the skeleton. In this case, you would provide a blank for the main heading, three blanks for

the subheadings, and space for the examples, as shown below. The key terms in this organizer are: *isosceles, right, square, heptagon, triangles, scalene, quadrilaterals, trapezoid, decagon, parallelogram, polygons, octagon, rhombus, pentagon, equilateral, hexagon.*

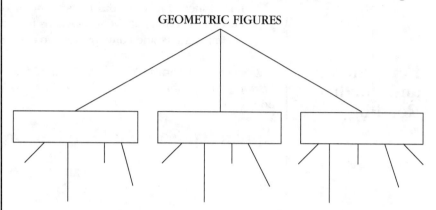

GEOMETRIC FIGURES

4. Have students work in pairs or individually to put the terms in a correct arrangement on the graphic organizer. (See Appendix for model.) Students may record terms in both English and their first language if they are at the beginning level. It is worth noting that understanding the plural *s* will help students distinguish between subconcepts and examples.
5. Discuss the students' completed organizers to clear up any misconceptions. Point out to students that depending upon the content, there may be no single correct arrangement.

Caveats and Options

1. Students may eventually design their own organizers to represent content.
2. Students may use the organizers as study guides and writing guides.
3. The discussion accompanying the construction of the organizers is a critical factor in learning.
4. Organizers are an excellent tool for ESL students to demonstrate understanding of key concepts when their command of the mechanics of English is still developing.

5. Graphic organizers can be used to represent a wide variety of content. For instance, the hierarchical graphic organizer could represent the branches of government and their components or the classification system in biology. Graphic organizers can take many forms, including Venn diagrams to point out similarities and differences; flow charts or cyclical designs to indicate cycles, processes, or chain reactions; and concept webs to explore specific topics or ideas.

References and Further Reading

Bromley, K., Irwin-DeVitis, L., & Modlo, M. (1995) *Graphic organizers: Visual strategy for active learning*. New York: Scholastic Professional Books.

Appendix: Sample Graphic Organizer

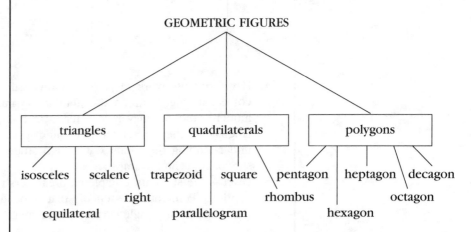

GEOMETRIC FIGURES

triangles — quadrilaterals — polygons

isosceles · scalene · right · equilateral

trapezoid · square · parallelogram · pentagon · rhombus

heptagon · decagon · hexagon · octagon

Contributor

Linda Irwin-DeVitis taught high school ESL in Louisiana and is currently a member of the reading and language arts faculty at Binghamton University, part of the State University of New York, in the United States.

Question Mapping for Science or Social Studies

Levels
Intermediate +

Aims
Ask questions and
pursue the answers
Practice higher level
cognitive thinking
Review key concepts
and related ideas
Connect material learned
(or to be learned) with
own lives
Practice speaking and
writing

Activity Type
Motivation, application,
review, or extension

Class Time
20-25 minutes at first,
10-15 minutes after a
few weeks' practice

Preparation Time
10-30 minutes

Resources
Poster or chart paper
Pencils/pens and note-
books for each student
Student work, library
books, science or social
studies visuals and realia,
displayed and accessible

This activity can be used in ESL, bilingual, or mainstream science or social studies classes, much as a KWL (know, want to know, learned) chart is used. It is most effective when frequently modeled and integrated at the beginning, middle, or end of an instructional activity.

Procedure

1. At a strategic point or the end of an activity (e.g., the discovery or observation of new data, a new process in science, or the careful viewing of a key visual in social studies), draw a circle on the chalkboard, with a key word, phrase, or idea written in the center. (Students can copy the circle and key word/phrase/idea in their notebooks.)

2. After the key idea is clear to all (via teacher or student clarification), draw lines outward from the circle, forming spokes around a wheel, with a circle attached to the end of each line. In each new circle around the wheel, write a different question word. The teacher, students, or both can determine what words these will be (e.g., *what, when, why, how*).

3. Organize the students into groups for the brainstorming step.

4. Ask groups to brainstorm and list questions about the key idea, especially new questions that have not come up in class discussion before or have not yet been satisfactorily answered. The questions may be related in a variety of ways to the key idea or may be personalized. Encourage students to think of questions that they really want to pursue.

5. After a set period of time, ask each group to pick a few of the best questions to share with the whole class. Write these in the circles surrounding the wheel on the chalkboard (or have the students write them). Assist students in clarifying and phrasing the questions,

so that all students understand them. (See sample question map in Appendix.)

6. After a full set of questions are listed on the map, have each student or small group copy the ones they are most interested in pursuing. As a new activity, they can pursue one question or several. Have them refer to student work on display, library books, textbooks, computer software, and other materials in the room as resources for inquiry. Encourage them also to take one question home each night, to find a person who can help answer it (e.g., family member, older peer, neighbor, local store owner, public worker, school personnel).

7. To assist with follow-up, ask students to use science or social studies journals to generate ideas, record questions, and keep track of their inquiry activities. These can be organized in a variety of ways, but students need to sense a sequence or process, which is often cyclic, of questioning, researching, recording answers, and generating new questions.

8. To make the students' questions visible over a period of days, ask students to make posters with their best questions, illustrated as needed to clarify key words, questions, and suggested routes of inquiry. New questions can be added to these posters, or miniposters can be made with new questions attached, as students find that one question leads to a better one, often a more concrete one that can more easily be pursued. A companion poster can be attached later entitled "Answers and Research Findings." On this poster, students can display ideas, examples, information, and graphics that reflect answers discovered during the inquiry process.

Caveats and Options

1. Take a few minutes before class to decide what key words, ideas, or concepts you may want to use. You could use several, assigning different ones to different groups of students.

2. The question map can be constructed by the whole class, with the teacher writing down questions given by students, or groups of students can work on their own maps, later sharing them with the whole class.

3. In Step 5, students may form new groups to pursue questions of shared interest.

4. To adapt this activity for beginners, teachers may want to translate the key question words into the students' native languages when possible, seeking help as needed from bilingual dictionaries, aides, parents, and adult native speakers.

5. After the teacher models the activity several times, students can suggest key words and ideas for the daily question mapping, or different groups of students can use different key words or ideas.

6. Some teachers and classes may prefer not to write the question word at all, leaving the circles around the key word blank until the brainstorming begins.

7. Students may be frustrated if their initial question is too broad to answer. Work with them to pare the question down to a reasonable level of inquiry.

8. Rather than using posters (or in addition to them), a three-ring binder or "class question book" can be left open in an accessible place, so that students can look at past question maps, add new questions more easily, and get ideas for new questions. The question book can make assessment of questioning activities more efficient and provide students with a sense of common, shared goals.

9. Check posters, journals, and question book frequently, to see if students are
   - asking questions related to the key word, idea, or concept, and showing some degree of understanding
   - using questions to connect content with their own concerns, interests, and lives
   - using more and more science or social studies language to ask questions and report on follow-up inquiry activities
   - asking questions at increasingly higher cognitive levels, showing an ability to "chain" questions from other questions, thus arriving at more specific, concrete, and researchable questions

10. Make brief notes for yourself after reading posters or the class question book for content needing more exemplification, clarification, or discussion in class. Also, observe and note which students seem to be more convergent or divergent or more abstract or concrete in their thinking and questioning skills, so that later question maps can provide practice for a wide variety of question types.

Appendix: Sample Question Mapping for Social Studies

Why do we have three branches of government?

Who is affected by these three branches of government everyday?

How am I affected by these three branches everyday?

When was the last time I was affected in my life by one of the branches?

Where can I go to find out more about one of these three branches?

The federal government is made up of three branches: executive, judicial, and legislative.

What happens if one of the branches has too much power?

When my dad says we shouldn't pay so many taxes or so much rent, what branch of government can we go to, to complain and do something about it?

When my mom gets sick and has to go to a special doctor, sometimes she says we can't afford it, because it's not covered. Where can she go to get help and which branch deals with this?

Contributor

Beti Leone prepares K-12 teachers for linguistically and culturally diverse classrooms, mentors bilingual student teachers, conducts research, and writes about language, learning, and teaching issues of bilingual students. She teaches and consults in California, in the United States.

Reading Across the Curriculum: A Genre-Based Perspective

Levels
Intermediate +; high school

Aims
Identify contextual features of written texts in different subject areas
Read and interpret text

Activity Type
Application

Class Time
1 hour

Preparation Time
15–30 minutes

Resources
Short written text from one of the students' subject areas
Reading worksheet

This genre-based perspective on reading will help students identify contextual features of texts and understand how they are written for the norms and expectations of a particular audience. This is useful for second language learners who read texts from a different cultural perspective and with different understandings and expectations from those of the writer and intended audience.

Procedure

1. Choose a short reading text from one of the students' subject areas.
2. Identify key contextual features of the text as per the categories presented in the worksheet in the Appendix.
3. Prepare pre-reading questions that focus on the main point(s) of the text and hand them out to the students before they begin to read.
4. Ask students to read the text to find answers to the comprehension questions.
5. Have students discuss their answers to the questions in pairs; then have a class discussion on the general content of the text.
6. Ask students to reread the text and, working together in pairs, identify key contextual features of the text, completing the worksheet provided in the Appendix.
7. As a class, discuss the context and perspective of the text. Ask students to take notes. Point out that most of the questions relate to the context of the text. The questions that refer to the perspective of the text are those related to its purpose, tone, and literal or nonliteral interpretation.
8. Ask students to write a short description of the text in which they describe the context and perspective of the text based on the notes they have taken in the previous step.

Caveats and Options

1. Ask students to examine texts from a number of different subject areas and discuss how different contextual components may lead to a different style and presentation of the texts.
2. Ask students to discuss how a text on the same topic might be presented in their own language and culture and to identify ways these texts might be similar or different from each other. They might consider, for example, the structural organization or whether the text would be read literally or figuratively.
3. Ask students to discuss how the text they have examined might change if one of the contextual components of the text were changed such as, having a different author, intended audience, purpose, or setting.
4. Analyze a text according to the categories presented in the Appendix. Then give the students the title and first paragraph of the text, together with your analysis, and ask them to construct a text on the same general topic.

References and Further Reading

Paltridge, B. (1995). Working with genre: A pragmatic perspective. *Journal of Pragmatics, 24,* 393–406.

Saville-Troike, M. (1989). The analysis of communicative events. In M. Saville-Troike (Ed.), *The ethnography of communication: An introduction* (2nd ed.) (pp. 107–180). Oxford: Basil Blackwell.

Appendix: Sample Reading Worksheet

Title of the text _____

What is the text about?	
What is the purpose of the text?	
What is the setting of the text? (e.g., in a textbook, a newspaper)	
What is the tone of the text? (e.g., formal, informal)	
Who is the author of the text?	
What is the author's age? sex? ethnic background? social status?	
Who is the intended audience of the text?	
What is the relationship between the author and intended audience of the text?	
What language is the text written in?	
What structural organization can you identify in the text? (e.g., its beginning, middle, and end)	
What rules or expectations limit how the text might be written?	
How would the text normally be interpreted? literally? figuratively?	
What shared cultural knowledge and understandings are implied in the text?	

Contributor

Brian Paltridge is a senior lecturer in applied linguistics at the University of Melbourne, in Australia. He has also taught ESL/EFL in New Zealand and Italy.

Pantomime It!

Levels
High beginning-
intermediate

Aims
Comprehend a reading
passage
Sequence events in a
reading passage
Be creative and act out
text
Think critically

Activity Type
Practice, application, or
review

Class Time
40–50 minutes

Preparation Time
10 minutes

Resources
Sentence strips of
reading passage
Materials for props (e.g.,
construction paper, glue,
scissors)

This activity helps students understand details in an academic reading passage. Student pairs pantomime a sentence from a passage that others try to identify and place in the story sequence.

Procedure

1. Select the passage students will read from a social studies book or a literary piece. Choose a reading passage with action. Write or type the sentences from the passage onto separate strips of paper.
2. Ask all the students to read the passage and discuss it briefly to be sure the class understands the main idea.
3. Pair students and give each pair one of the sentence strips. Ask each pair to plan a pantomime to reflect the content of the strip. The pairs may make or use props if desired.
4. Give students time to practice.
5. Call pairs up to the front of the class to perform, out of sequence. After each pair performs the pantomime twice, ask the nonperforming pairs to read through the passage and identify the sentence which has just been pantomimed.
6. Have the nonperforming pairs share their decisions. You may want to ask them to justify their selections. Record these decisions on the board to check later.
7. Continue this process until all the pairs have performed. Review the guesses from the board and identify which ones were correct.
8. Once all the groups have completed their pantomimes, organize a class pantomime of the reading passage. Have all pairs stand along a side wall in order and perform their pantomimes of the story in sequence.

Caveats and Options

1. If desired, pantomime groups may consist of three or four students, especially if the sentence includes multiple characters.
2. Some strips may contain two sentences if the action is closely linked.
3. The activity may be planned for two periods over 2 days. The first day the student pairs plan and practice their pantomime. For homework they can gather or make props. The second day, they perform.
4. Another option is to assign points for correct guesses. The pair that guesses the most pantomimed sentences correctly wins. If desired, two points could be assigned for an exact guess, one point for a reasonable guess (based on the quality of the pantomime and the pair's justification for their sentence selection).
5. This activity might also be used to describe scientific processes, experiments, and conclusions in a science class.

References and Further Readings

Short, D., Montone, C., Frekot, S., & Elfin, A. (1996). Inca unit. *Conflicts in world cultures*. Washington, DC: Center for Applied Linguistics.

Contributor

Deborah Short conducts research on integrated language and content instruction at the Center for Applied Linguistics, in Washington, DC. She has taught ESL/EFL in California, New York, and Virginia, in the United States, and in the Congo (Zaire).

Flags: Symbols of Protest

Levels
Intermediate +; middle school

Aims
Review U.S. revolutionary groups
Create a symbolic flag
Work cooperatively
Practice speaking and inferencing

Activity Type
Assessment or culminating project

Class Time
2-3 days

Preparation Time
1 hour

Resources
Handout showing sample flags
Flag design worksheet
Mural paper or other large paper for painting
Paints and brushes

In this activity, students use their knowledge of the different groups active during the American Revolution to design an imaginary flag by choosing symbols to represent one of the groups.

Procedure

1. Before this lesson, have several students draw flags of their native countries. Begin the lesson with the students presenting their flags to the class and have the class brainstorm what the symbols on the flags may represent.
2. Have students look at several pre-Revolutionary flags from colonial America, and analyze what the symbols mean. (See Appendix A for sample.)
3. Divide class into groups of two, three, or four and ask each group to design a flag for one of the groups in the Revolution, choosing from the following: Sons of Liberty, Daughters of Liberty, Minutemen, Loyalists, Native Americans, African Americans (slaves or free), Dutch traders, or neutral colonists. Distribute the flag worksheet (see Appendix B) to have students design the group flag, using appropriate symbols to reflect the group. It may be helpful to model the worksheet with the class before the groups design their own.
4. Have students paint their flags on mural paper.
5. Students can present their flags to the class, explaining why they chose their symbols. Prior to their explanation, other students can guess the meaning of the symbols.
6. Students can write their flag title and an explanation of the flag symbols on an index card. Attach both to the flag for display on a bulletin board in the classroom, hallway, or school library.

Caveats and Options

1. Students can look in newspapers and magazines for flags or banners of protest related to issues in the news. Discuss the meanings of the symbols.
2. Students may conduct research on their own country's flag: Were there earlier designs? What do the symbols and colors stand for?
3. Students can illustrate and describe state flags.
4. Students can sew a flag, perhaps in conjunction with a home economics or life skills class.
5. This activity can be used in relation to other historical time periods where several groups played roles in major events.
6. This activity can be a team-building task for student groups.

References and Further Reading

Short, D., Mahrer, C., Liten-Tejada, R., Elfin, A., & Montone, C. (1994). *Protest and the American Revolution: An integrated language, social studies and culture unit for middle school American History.* Washington, DC: Center for Applied Linguistics.

Appendix A: Sample Flag Graphics

Appendix B: Sample Worksheet, Revolutionary Protest Flags

Design a Revolutionary Protest Flag Worksheet

Group Name: _____

Background color of flag: _____

Stands for: _____

Symbol:	Color:	Stands for:
_____	_____	_____
_____	_____	_____
_____	_____	_____
_____	_____	_____

Draw a rough draft of your flag:

Contributor

Robin Liten-Tejada has taught social studies, science, math, and language arts in the secondary HILT (High Intensity Language Training) Program in Virginia, in the United States for more than 10 years.

How Big Is It Anyway?

Levels
Intermediate; middle school

Aims
Review measurement
Bring height and length into relative terms
Prepare for a geography unit
Understand distance
Practice sequence writing and comparisons

Activity Type
Motivation or practice

Class Time
50 minutes

Preparation Time
1-3 hours

Resources
Chart of rivers and mountains (or other landforms or landmarks)
Rulers, calculators
Bags of peanut M&Ms

This activity can be used to introduce landforms or waterways of a new country being studied. Measuring an everyday item helps the student visualize the magnitude of mountains or rivers more accurately.

Procedure

1. Prepare a list of four to six major landforms of your next area of study (e.g., China). Have students make a chart or complete one that you give them to record the length or height of the landforms (in miles) using the *World Almanac*. (See Appendix.)
2. Once the students have completed recording the lengths or heights, have them calculate the miles into feet (be sure they show their work and double-check with a calculator).
3. Divide students into groups of four or five and distribute one ruler and one bag of peanut M&Ms. Have the groups place all of the M&Ms from the bag in a line and carefully measure the line (it should measure almost exactly 1 foot).
4. Once they complete the measurement, have the groups determine how many bags of M&Ms it would take to line the "Great Wall" or a landform or waterway suitable to your study topic.
5. When the chart is complete, have the groups write the procedure they used to find the answers to Step 4 on a sequence chart or in narrative format.

Caveats and Options

1. This activity may be broadened to include more math and social studies skills, but it would then become a 2–3 day lesson. Creating

papier mâché mountains, for social studies, or studying proportions, for math, lend themselves nicely as follow-up activities.

2. If necessary, plan a prior lesson to review how to use an almanac with students.

3. This activity is designed for students with functional math skills. In multilevel classes, or with less proficient students, you might prepare some copies of the chart with the lengths and heights already researched (e.g., the miles column completed) for them to use. You may also want to model the process with one of the landforms.

4. If desired, student groups could use objects other than peanut M&Ms. If students have difficulty with decimals, try to find something that measures to a round distance (e.g., licorice strips).

Appendix: Sample Measurement Chart for China

Places	Miles	Feet	No. of Bags of M&Ms
South China Sea	895,400		
Huang Ho	2,900		
Xi River	1,236		
Gobi Desert	500,000		

Contributor

Sally Frekot has taught middle school social studies for 10 years in Maryland, in the United States. She has coauthored an ESL social studies curriculum unit on world cultures.

Supply and Demand

Levels
Intermediate

Aims
Learn economic
definitions of supply
and demand
Use definitions to
predict prices
Practice listening and
writing

Activity Type
Motivation

Class Time
50 minutes

Preparation Time
1–3 hours

Resources
Product to sell
Play money
Overhead transparency
or copies of worksheet
Pictures from magazines

This activity may be used as a springboard to an economics unit or prior to a lesson on communism. The selling of your product attracts the students' attention.

Procedure

1. Depending on the time of your class and season, bring in six products to sell to your class (e.g., for hot days, ice cold sodas; a morning class, cream-filled donuts).
2. Distribute play money, $5 per student.
3. Hold up your first item. Explain how wonderful it is and why you have only a few (e.g., the factory was destroyed, storm ruined the cocoa crop) and ask one student if he or she would like to purchase it for $1. Be sure you choose a student who will ham it up to increase the class frenzy. After the first sale, continue to sell the remaining products at higher and higher prices. Do not suggest the students pool their money, but allow it if they conceive of the idea. You may use that concept in a later lesson in the unit, or depending on your unit objectives, the concepts of mergers, monopolies and pooling money may be introduced now.
4. As you sell your products, permit students to consume the product immediately because this encourages the "market." After all items are sold, distribute the handout or use an overhead transparency (see Appendix).
5. Have students work as a class or in pairs to generate a definition that they will remember for the vocabulary words the class has been working on, and an explanation of how each term affects the other, using your demonstration as a reference.

6. Continue with the situations on the handout and have students write solutions for each one.
7. You can also hold up pictures of things that may influence supply and demand (e.g., storms, bugs, a famous celebrity endorsing a product) for your closure. As you hold up the picture, students can write a sentence on what and how a product might be influenced. For example:
   - Hold up a picture of a bug on a plant. Ask the class, "How could insects raise the price of oranges?"
   - Hold up a picture of Michael Jordan on a cereal box. "How might Michael Jordan cause other cereal prices to go down?"
8. Ask students to select a product to follow. Instruct students to keep a journal on their product for several months. For the first entry, have them note the product and the date, place, and price of purchase. They should continue to note sales, endorsements, or anything else that may influence the price, and they should also record changes in price. Periodically, ask students to report on their products to the class.

Caveats and Options

1. If desired, write more "What If . . ." situation cards and distribute or have student groups write their own.
2. This activity may be adapted to a lower proficiency level by supplying the beginning phrase for answers and completing the activity together on the overhead.
3. You could make the lesson more challenging by having the students read news articles that deal with the lesson topic and explain (in writing) how international events may affect the local economy.

Appendix: Sample Handout

Supply and Demand

Define:

Supply:

Demand:

Explain: What happens to prices when . . .

1. supply is up, but demand is down?

2. supply is down, but demand is up?

What would you do if . . . ?

1. your store ordered too many oranges and you had to sell them before they went bad?

2. you owned the only store in town that sold tennis shoes?

3. you lived in a city where it never snowed? What products could you sell at high prices? What products would not sell at all?

4. you needed to choose the perfect product to sell to this class?

Contributor

Sally Frekot has taught middle school social studies for 10 years in Maryland, in the United States. She has coauthored an ESL social studies curriculum unit on world cultures.

Jigsaw Field Trips in ESL Social Studies

Levels
Any; high school

Aims
Review orally content
information learned on
a field trip
Apply individual
knowledge to a
cooperative group
activity

Activity Type
Application or review

Class Time
One–three periods to
prepare for and take
field trip
One–three periods for
cooperative group
activity

Preparation Time
1–2 hours

Resources
Expert sheets
Field trip information
and materials
Notebooks for students

This activity allows each student to apply information learned on a field trip through a group task. Students share individual information and perspectives, discuss new or difficult vocabulary, and interpret or construct what they experienced through a cooperative activity.

Procedure

1. Organize a field trip making necessary arrangements (e.g., plan to visit a bank or financial institution, make an appointment with bank contact person, collect parental permission forms, select transportation). Prepare listings of expert and home groups. Students should be divided into six expert groups: two A groups, two B groups, and two C groups. Home groups should consist of one A, one B, and one C student from these expert groups.
2. Visit the field trip site to obtain data to formulate expert sheets (see Appendix A) and prepare the review quiz.
3. Orient the class to the field trip briefly (e.g., an activity in conjunction with unit on Money and Financial Institutions), emphasizing key areas on which students should focus. Explain to students that they will need to take notes as appropriate, and collect materials or handouts on the field trip if they are available.
4. Go on the field trip.
5. The next day, organize students into the six expert groups. Distribute expert sheets A, B, C to the appropriate groups. Arrange the classroom in circular desk groups to promote face-to-face interaction among students. If desired, post a listing of the expert and home groups.
6. Explain the procedures to be followed (see Appendix B). If the class has prior cooperative learning experience, the explanation need only

be a quick review and could be provided on a handout or posted on the board.

7. Allot about 25–30 minutes for the expert groups to complete their assigned expert sheets using recall information, their notes, and handouts or materials obtained from the field trip.

8. Next, organize students into the home groups. Have home group experts teach each other their information following the order of the expert sheets (A, B, C) for about 25–35 minutes. Students may use blank expert sheets or take notes to compile the shared knowledge of the group members. Students are to follow procedures outlined in the learning of the material. Monitor group behaviors closely and act as a facilitator during the process.

9. The next day, have students complete a quick review quiz with questions drawn from the expert sheets. This provides the teacher with an individual assessment of each student's learning for account-ability purposes.

Caveats and Options

1. This activity focuses on a field trip to a local bank branch by an ESL Free Enterprise or Economics class. The activity can be adapted and modified for many different settings (e.g., a visit to a grocery store, an insurance company, an eatery, a hotel, or a group viewing of a film at a cinema).

2. The preparation time allotted is based on the assumption that the teacher is already familiar with the site to be visited.

3. The length of the trip, number of expert sheets, and group assignments can be modified to accommodate a particular class size or proficiency level.

4. The orientation can be done prior to the field trip. The quiz is usually most appropriate after students have been given individual review time. It is not meant to be a period-long assessment.

5. If this lesson is part of a continuing expert/home group cooperative learning process, bonus points can be awarded to home groups based on individual quiz scores. During this activity students may also receive points based on their use of cooperative group skills. (I do not give points for completed expert sheets.)

Appendix A: Sample Expert Sheet A

Field Trip to Bank/Financial Institution

Answer the following questions using information/knowledge obtained from our field trip to Norwest Bank.

1. What is a *teller line*? What role does a *teller* have in a bank?
2. Name three different kinds of bank accounts a customer can open at the *new accounts* desk.
3. What is an *ATM*? At the bank branch we visited, where are the ATMs?
4. Describe the system of drive-up teller lanes.
5. What type of utility payments can a customer make at the bank branch we visited?

[Note: Expert Sheets B and C can ask questions pertaining to the vault, safety deposit boxes, loan office, credit cards, customer service phone line, bookkeeping, records, notary public service, investments office, and the bank computer system.]

Appendix B: Cooperative Group Procedures

1. Organize quickly into your assigned expert groups (see posting).
2. While completing the expert sheets, answer the questions together. Each group member must agree that the answer is correct before moving on to the next question. Stay within your group.
3. Ask the teacher questions for clarification or assistance only if no one in your group is able to provide guidance or focus for the group.
4. Upon completion of expert sheets, plan how information will be presented in home groups and then review the information together to ensure mastery of the material.
5. Organize quickly into your assigned home groups (see posting).
6. Teach each other the information following the order of expert sheets (A, B, C).
7. Review, quiz, and discuss the information with each other to ensure mastery of the material.

Contributor

Juan M. Armijo is a social studies teacher at Camelback High School in Arizona, in the United States. His interests include civic education, politics, and alternative forms of assessment.

Searching for Clues: Using Scavenger Hunts To Enhance Language Learning

Levels
Intermediate +

Aims
Review vocabulary
Identify and define
people, events, and
objects
Practice writing

Activity Type
Presentation of
information or review

Class Time
3 hours

Preparation Time
2-3 hours

Resources
Museum or gallery

This activity is designed to help students describe, define, and explain the important elements of a museum or gallery.

Procedure

Before Class:

1. Select a museum or gallery that is related to the course content, a particular unit, theme, or lesson.
2. Decide in advance what information the students should be familiar with and the questions students should be able to answer.
3. Spend a few hours at the museum or gallery looking for a very large variety of terms, pictures, objects, paintings, books, and artifacts related to your objectives. Make a list of all of these items.
4. Divide the list into themes. The themes can be related to historical periods, modes of presentation, rooms in the museum or gallery, and so forth.
5. Create a scavenger-hunt form by organizing the items, or questions about the items, according to the themes. (See Appendix.)
6. Assign points to each item on the scavenger hunt.

During Class:

7. The day before going to the museum or gallery give the students the scavenger hunt form in class and review the directions with them.
8. Take students to the museum or gallery.
9. Have students search for the answers to the questions or items on the scavenger hunt
10. Ask students to present their findings to the entire class.

Caveats and Options

1. Make several different versions of a scavenger hunt form so students hunt for different information.
2. Provide clipboards to facilitate writing.
3. Students may work together in pairs or triads on a single scavenger hunt.
4. Teachers with lower level students may modify the questions so that they are easier or more comprehensible for the students. Teachers with a mixed-level class may design different scavenger hunt forms for different proficiency levels.
5. Include only as many question on the scavenger hunt as students can answer in the amount of time allocated at the museum or gallery. The time will vary according to the amount of detail expected for each answer, the students' abilities, and the complexity of the question; however, a list of 10–15 items is recommended.

Appendix: Sample Scavenger Hunt at an Historical Museum

Vocabulary. Identify and give examples of the following terms:

> *civil rights movement*
> *boycott*

People. Who were the following historical figures? Why are they famous? What did they do?

> Malcolm X
> Dr. Martin Luther King, Jr.
> Rosa Parks
> John F. Kennedy

Events. Describe and explain the important events that happened in the following places. How did they affect history?

> Montgomery, Alabama, 1955
> Washington, DC, August 28, 1963. Who spoke at this event?

Contributor

Maya Alvarez-Galvan taught ESL in high school in California, in the United States, and is working on her PhD at the University of Southern California.

Meet a Tree

Levels
Intermediate +

Aims
Practice speaking,
observation, and drawing
skills
Write a journal entry
Integrate science with
ESL
Think creatively

Activity Type
Practice or application

Class Time
50 minutes

Preparation Time
10 minutes

Resources
Colored pencils, drawing
paper, notebook paper,
pencil, magnifying glass

This activity integrates science with ESL and provides students with the opportunity for a field trip outside the school. It requires an area with enough trees so each pair of students can study one.

Procedure

1. Begin a class discussion by reviewing facts that students know about trees. List these points on the board or make a word web of *Trees*.
2. Ask, "If you were looking at a particular tree, what are some questions you would ask about it?" Write these on the board.
3. Divide students into pairs. Assign one to be the recorder and one to be the artist.
4. Tell students they will be observing a tree today. Allow time for students to write down questions about the tree. These questions will help guide their investigations during this activity.
5. Distribute materials. Ask each pair to section off a piece of drawing paper into eight squares, by first folding it in half horizontally, then folding it in half vertically, and then in half vertically again. Demonstrate. They will use this paper to sketch their observations.
6. Explain the activity. Students will go outside and each pair will select a tree to study.
   ● The pairs will observe everything they can about the tree, but they are not to pull off leaves, bark, any animal, or any other thing.
   ● Students will refer to the questions they wrote; the recorders will write as many answers as the pair knows or can discover. Students should write new questions if they think of them. They should write down all the information they can about the tree while observing it.

- The artists are to draw an aspect of the tree on the drawing paper, one item per square. Sketches need to be labeled and colored.

7. Go outside and let each pair of students select a tree and work on the task. Circulate to help guide the observations.
8. When students are finished, either return to the classroom or take a "tree tour" outside so pairs can share their tree with the rest of the class.
9. Have each student write a journal entry on a piece of notebook paper. Write questions on the board that suggest journal entries: *What new facts did you learn about a tree? What did you think about the tree? How did you find the answers to your questions? What other questions did you think of? Do you have any unanswered questions? How well did your team work together?*
10. Each group turns in the recorded questions and answers and the drawing page. Individuals turn in their journal writing.

Caveats and Options

1. Students can view their trees during different seasons and repeat this activity.
2. Students often ask how to find the height of the tree. They can easily find out using a protractor, straw, and a string with a weight (see *Wonder Science*, November, 1994, from the American Chemical Society, 1155 16th Street, NW, Washington, DC 22036 USA).

References and Further Reading

Moutran, J.S. (1990). *Elementary science activities for all seasons*. West Nyack, NY: The Center for Applied Research in Education.

Contributor

Joan M. Dungey has taught ESL at all levels and is the curriculum coordinator at Yellow Springs High School. She also teaches in the languages and literature department at Cedarville College, and in the education department at the MacGregor School of Antioch University, in Ohio, in the United States.

Food Groups Interactive Bulletin Board

Levels
Beginning; middle school

Aims
Categorize foods into food groups
Review vocabulary
Practice reading and speaking

Activity Type
Practice or assessment

Class Time
50 minutes

Preparation Time
30 minutes

Resources
Magazines, newspapers
Scissors
Bulletin board, pins

Students work together, using listening and speaking skills, to create an interactive bulletin board about food groups, selecting items themselves. Items can be added, moved, or changed to introduce, reinforce, or supplement different aspects of the topic.

Procedure

1. Set up a bulletin board in a chart format with the title, Food Groups, and columns labeled Fruits and Vegetables, Breads and Grains, Dairy, and Meat/Poultry. A Sweets column is optional.
2. Discuss nutrition. Explain the role of the U.S. Department of Agriculture (USDA). Describe the USDA's "approved" food groups and recommended daily amounts. Discuss the food categories.
3. Provide newspaper food supplements or magazines with pictures of foods. Ask students to cut out their choice of foods and put them in the proper categories on the bulletin board.
4. After the bulletin board is full, lead a class discussion analyzing the categories.

Caveats and Options

1. Let students write family menus which use all the food groups with balanced meals.
2. Extend the study into math by adding prices from the newspaper supplements to the bulletin board. Then analyze the costs of the different food groups on the board.
3. Use the bulletin board for vocabulary assessment by pinning numbers on foods from the class vocabulary list and asking students to write down the names of the items.

4. If this activity is done on a hall bulletin board, the ESL program will attract schoolwide attention.
5. If you do not have a bulletin board available, use a portable free-standing one of cardboard or insulation foam (available at home improvement stores) or use a large piece of paper or poster board.

References and Further Reading

Dungey, J.M. (1989). *Interactive bulletin boards as teaching tools*. Washington, DC: National Education Association.

Contributor

Joan M. Dungey has taught ESL at all levels and is the curriculum coordinator at Yellow Springs High School. She also teaches in the languages and literature Department at Cedarville College, and in the education department at the MacGregor School of Antioch University, in Ohio, in the United States.

Daily Math Journal: What Did I Learn, and How Can I Use It?

Levels
High beginning +

Aims
Recognize daily learning
progress
Practice self-reflection
and self-evaluation
strategies
Review math concepts
and processes
Practice writing

Activity Type
Assessment or review

Class Time
10-15 minutes at first,
then 5-10 minutes after
a few week's practice

Preparation Time
15-30 minutes

Resources
Pencils or pens and
notebooks for each
student
List of math concepts
covered in class
Other math visuals or
realia used in class each
day

This activity may be done at the end of an ESL math or mainstream math class. It is most effective when initially taught and modeled as an activity integrated into instruction at a strategic point in the daily lesson, such as after students have learned a new concept or applied a concept to an authentic problem-solving situation.

Procedure

1. Ask students to bring a math notebook or journal to class every day.
2. While conducting a lesson on a given math concept, stop at a strategic point—after all students seem to have understood a topic or concept—and ask them to take a minute to answer two questions in their journals: What did I learn about math today? How can I use what I learned outside of math class (e.g., at home, on the job, in recreation, in other classes).
3. Practice this procedure every day for a week, always stopping at a strategic point in the lesson to let students answer the same two questions. Encourage students to use visuals to accompany their answers.
4. After 1-2 weeks, when you feel certain that all students have learned to answer the two questions at the strategic stopping point, explain to them that you will now allow time at the end of each class for them to answer the two daily questions in their math journals.
5. Provide time for students to share their journals periodically so that they can see what they are learning and hear about their classmates' learning too. If students are hesitant at first to share, try reading some journal entries aloud (anonymously) and express satisfaction about what students have learned and their good ideas.

Caveats and Options

1. Before each class, decide on the strategic point at which you will stop the lesson and ask students to reflect in their journals. Determine if this point will bring about the most success for all students.

2. Be sure to check the journals each day to monitor student progress in three areas:
   - Are the students using reflective language?
   - Are the students talking about math in their answers?
   - Are the students expanding their "math talk" each day to include more detail, more higher level thinking, and more enthusiasm?

3. You may want to keep your own journal and write in it at the same time as the students.

4. Make brief notes daily for yourself, after reading the students' math journals, with ideas for the following day—ways to elicit the three points above or improve other features, while at the same time supporting students and acknowledging their successes in math and in the journals.

5. By reading these journals, you can also determine if there are any misconceptions or misunderstandings in your students' math knowledge. Knowing what your students understand or do not understand provides you with information for exploring and correcting any misconceptions and misunderstandings in subsequent classes.

6. To encourage students to ask and answer their own questions about math, begin a new cycle in which you again stop at a strategic point but offer two new questions. Allow the class to choose one question to answer so that a decision must be made and negotiations must go on about which question is best, most interesting, easiest, or hardest. At other times, each pair or group of students could choose one of the two questions to answer, again pushing them to think about how we ask questions. Cycle questions weekly (or daily) and use the opportunity to discuss:
   - What different kinds of questions can we ask?
   - Which question types could help us understand and solve this problem?
   - What kinds of notes and graphics can help us?

These discussions will help students see the importance of diverse thinking (i.e., different types of questions and various ways of solving problems).

7. Open discussion about which are questions we really want or need to find answers to, encouraging lateral and creative thinking about math in everyday situations. (See Appendix.) After students are familiar with question types, encourage them to ask and answer their own questions in their journals. These student-generated questions could be presented or written down for the entire class, perhaps on a daily "Math Questions" poster where one student lists a new question per day. Then, the class could enter into a discussion about that question, thus modeling or practicing the creative thinking that such questions stimulate.

References and Further Reading

National Council of Teachers of Mathematics. (1989). *Curriculum and evaluation standards for school mathematics*. Reston, VA: Author.

Appendix: Sample Creative Questions

1. Probability (7th-grade math)

   - What are the chances that my English teacher will call on me in class today, in a 45-minute period, when the teacher's usual practice (her goal) is to call on everyone at least five times a week, and the class meets four times a week?

   - Two ancillary questions might be: What pieces of information do I need to find out the answer? and Would an estimate be sufficient for this question or situation? (For more ideas, see National Council of Teachers of Mathematics, 1989, pp.109–111.)

2. Connections with Other Disciplines (11th-grade math)

   - When I go out to warm up the car at 7 a.m. in January when the temperature is 15° Fahrenheit, how can math help me solve (or predict) the problems that can come up? These problems include: (a) the door lock is frozen; (b) the car won't start; (c) the car needs to warm up; (d) the windshield is covered with ice; and (e) caution is needed to avoid an accident (due to weather) on the way to school.

● Two ancillary questions might be: What effect do heat, force, time, and humidity have in each of these situations? and What graphic analysis can I make for each question and what equation might I write for each question?" (For more ideas, see National Council of Teachers of Mathematics, 1989, pp. 146–149.)

Contributor

Beti Leone teaches in the Department of Linguistics, California State University, Fresno, in the United States, preparing K-12 teachers for linguistically and culturally diverse classrooms and conducting research and writing on bilingual issues.

Content Concentration

Levels
Any

Aims
Develop learning
strategies
Practice a memory aid
Review content
information

Activity Type
Application or review

Class Time
20–30 minutes

Preparation Time
15–30 minutes

Resources
3-in. x 5-in. or larger
index cards
Prizes for winners
(optional)

Content Concentration can be used to teach students mnemonic strategies, as well as to help students learn facts or review factual knowledge. It can be used to study content or vocabulary knowledge in any discipline.

Procedure

1. Prepare a set of paired information cards. (Sixteen cards is a good number to introduce students to the game.) The pairs might be something like: word and definition, symbol and meaning, famous person's name and reason for fame, city and state. (See Appendix.) The playing surface could be a group of student desks if you plan to have several small groups playing at once, or the blackboard with the cards held up with tape or magnets if you play with the whole class.
2. Shuffle the cards and lay them out in a grid pattern, with the written information face down.
3. Label the rows with letters and the columns with numbers. The letters and numbers allow the students to call out the card they want, for example, "A1" or "D3".
4. Place the students on teams, or let them play individually. If there are several groups, photocopy the first set of cards to save writing time. If you have a lot of factual information to be studied or reviewed, place separate sets of cards at different tables and permit the students to rotate.
5. The students begin by calling out a card, "A1" or "E4," and a designated person turns it over for a moment. The same student then calls out a second card. If the cards match, the student takes the cards and gets one point. If the cards do not match, they are turned face down once again. The next student then chooses cards and tries to make a match.

Other students, meanwhile, try to develop ways to remember where specific cards are, so that when their turn comes, they can get the match.

6. When all the matches are made, the team with the most points wins. A small prize may increase the students' desire to remember the match, and thus the factual information as well.

Caveats and Options

1. Once the Content Concentration cards are made, they can be used by individual students who need further work with the factual information. They could be part of a learning center activity in which students would match the cards using their books and notebooks if necessary.

2. Students could use the cards as a model to create their own vocabulary cards, matching information such as word and definition.

3. Cards used for learning about the metric system could be matched to items in the science class that use the same particular measurement, such as beakers, droppers, rulers, and balance.

4. The cards for the Events of the Revolutionary War could include longer examples. For example, the "Battle of Yorktown" card could read "Battle of Yorktown—Washington attacked the British stationed there by land and the French navy attacked by sea. The British surrendered." The cards, then, could help the students remember why each event was important.

5. The cards for the Events of the Revolutionary War could also be used to make a human timeline. Each student would get a matched set of cards. Lining up in the classroom, they would try to find their place in history by getting into the proper place chronologically.

6. For students less familiar with the "A1" or "E2" concept, you could put a number on the back of each card and have the students select the card by number.

7. Beginning-level students or students with limited formal schooling could use the cards to create a sentence.

Appendix: Sample Content Concentration Game Boards

Below are several examples of content-based concentration boards. This game can be applied to any level of school and any content area. The index cards can also be used for other purposes once they are made.

Topic: Math Symbols

	1	2	3	4
A	is less than	=	$\sqrt{}$	percent
B	+	divided by	is greater than	$\leq$
C	is less than or equal to	plus	−	$\geq$
D	%	minus	>	÷
E	equals	the square root of	is greater than or equal to	<

Topic: Metric System Prefixes

	1	2	3	4
A	mega	hecto	the basic unit (equal to 39 inches)	one thousand times the basic unit
B	ten times the basic unit	one-tenth (1/10) of the basic unit	milli	one-thousandth (1/1000) of the basic unit
C	(no prefix)	one-hundredth (1/100) of the basic unit	one million times the basic unit	centi
D	one hundred times the basic unit	kilo	deci	deca

Topic: Events in the American Revolutionary War

	1	2	3	4	5
A	1765	April 19, 1775	Battle of Yorktown	1774	September 1783
B	October 1781	Boston Massacre	The Declaration of Independence was signed.	Boston Tea Party	February 1778
C	The battles of Lexington and Concord	July 4, 1776	Treaty of Paris	France enters the war.	1773
D	1770	Intolerable Acts	Winter of 1777–1778	Stamp Act	Winter at Valley Forge

Contributor

Emily Lynch Gómez has been in the ESL/EFL profession for more than 10 years. She currently works at the Center for Applied Linguistics, in Washington, DC, in the United States, on the ESL Standards and Assessment project.

◆ Survival and Career Orientation

How Do I Get There?

Levels
High beginning-
intermediate

Aims
Learn directional
vocabulary and phrases
Become comfortable
asking for assistance
when traveling
Internalize patterns *How
do I/you get to . . . ?, How
long does it take you/
will it take me . . . ?*

Activity Type
Presentation of
information or practice

Class Time
1 hour

Preparation Time
40 minutes

Resources
Poster depicting an urban
area with clearly drawn
streets, intersections, road
signs, and some
communal places
Additional set of cardboard
road signs and street lights
Toy car and two telephones

This activity may be used to develop communication skills necessary to give and understand directions as well as to teach trip planning skills.

Procedure

1. Ask students if they have recently visited some new places like shopping centers, libraries, movie theaters, or a new friend's home, and if so, how they got there: Did they drive, take a bus or metro, get a ride, or walk? Ask if they had good directions and could easily find the place. Say that today they are going to learn how to give and understand directions.

2. Place a poster of an urban area on the board and begin to introduce new vocabulary, such as: *go straight, make a left turn, traffic light, stay in the right lane, intersection, gas station, stop sign, block, eastbound/northbound*, illustrating the meaning of the terms with toy car movements and the poster.

3. Place the car at "home" on the poster and ask the students how the driver can get to different places on the poster—the post office, library, hotel, gas station. Modify assignments by fixing on the poster additional cardboard destinations and road signs.

4. Tell students that their next task will be to guess a certain place in the school neighborhood by the directions that you are going to give them. Read directions and have students try to guess the place. When they successfully perform this task, suggest that they make up their own puzzles.

5. Undertake a discussion of traveling time. You may want to underline punctuality as an essential U.S. cultural norm and ask students how they perceive it: "Is it very important in your country to be on time? If you have to arrive at a certain time, would it be considered impolite if you are 10, 15, or 20 minutes late?" Tell the students that because it is very important to be able to estimate traveling time to a new place, they may want to ask about the time they are likely to need to make the trip when asking for directions.

6. Introduce the pattern *How long will it take me to get there?* Explain that *how long?* means *how much time?* and that *it* stands for the travel. Have students practice this pattern in different tenses. For example, you can say and write a sentence on the board: "Last Sunday I drove to New York." Encourage students to ask: "How long did it take you to get there?" When students master this question, have them practice with answers: "It took me. . . . or, It will take you/him/her. . . ."

7. Tell students that despite having maps and directions, some people still get lost. Ask what they would do in such a situation. After they respond and share ideas, explain that stopping at a gas station is the most common way for Americans to seek traveling assistance. Suggest that someone has stopped at a gas station and needs some help with directions. How should he address the attendant? Try to elicit answers from the students and then practice: "How can I get to . . . ?"

8. Now have your students create and dramatize their own dialogues, first asking for directions on the telephone, then seeking assistance at a gas station.

Caveats and Options

1. For more advanced students, this activity may be carried out with real local maps. Students would be asked to prepare directions between two given places.

2. Students may have difficulty using object forms of personal pronouns in the pattern "It takes me/him/her/us/them . . . ." To avoid common mistakes, a review of subject and object forms may be helpful.

References and Further Reading

Rivers, W.M. (1987). *Interactive language teaching*. New York: Cambridge University Press.

Billings, H. (1993). *Maps—globes—graphs*. Austin, TX: Steck-Vaughn.

Contributor

Jane Toverovskaia immigrated to the United States from Russia. She taught adult ESL in Florida, and currently teaches ESL in Bryant Alternative High School, in Virginia, in the United States.

Reading Any Map

Levels
Beginning–intermediate

Aims
Practice making choices
Read maps of different
kinds
Review map symbols
Follow directions

Activity Type
Application or review

Class Time
2 hours

Preparation Time
15 minutes

Resources
Approximately 30 maps
of different kinds

In this open-ended, multilevel activity, students practice map reading skills in a relaxed, enjoyable setting. It is a culminating review and reinforcement activity for a map-reading study and generates a lot of oral discussion among students.

Procedure

1. Collect a variety of maps, including political maps, relief maps, street maps; maps of the ocean floor, space, and fantasy lands (which are especially interesting if based on the students' literature, such as Narnia, Oz, Middle Earth, Pern); and specialty maps (e.g., bicycle trails, national parks, mazes). Put them in an easily accessible place for student use. If possible, laminate them so they last longer.

2. Before beginning this activity, teach selected map skills. Review the following vocabulary words: *title* (students need to know that maps need a title), *compass rose, cardinal directions (N, NW, W, SW, S, SE, E, NE), key, legend, scale, symbols.*

3. Give each student a handout. (See Appendix.) Read the directions together. Explain the vocabulary. The questions are "generic," that is, applicable to any map. Some maps may not have all items referred to in the questions. Tell students what to do if their map does not have an item (e.g., put *NA* for *not applicable*).

4. Show students the procedure of selecting a map and laying it flat on a table (or the floor). If necessary, especially for beginners, model the assignment with one map before students work individually. Students also may work in pairs of you wish.

5. Circulate throughout the room, helping students fill out the questions as they work through the handout. Explain any new or unusual symbols on the maps.

6. After the students have completed the activity, let each one explain to the class or in small groups which map they liked best.

Caveats and Options

1. You may set a minimum number of maps to examine or encourage students to work on as many as possible in the time provided. You may want to make multiple copies of the handout per student.
2. Let students draw maps of the route from their homes to school and write the directions for others to read.
3. Consider assigning a writing activity which would include drawing a map to help to understand the setting of a story (e.g., science fiction, mystery).

References and Further Reading

1. Maps can be found at used bookstores and in *National Geographic* magazines. Community members may donate collections of old *National Geographic* magazines with maps in them. Ask automobile club members for their old maps. Check with people going on vacation and ask them to bring back maps for you. Gathering a wide variety of maps may take time.
2. Suggested video series: "Understanding Maps" and "Using Maps" from the video series *Using Maps, Globes, Graphs, and Tables.* United Learning (6633 W. Howard St., Niles, IL 60648 USA. Tel. 800-759-0362 [from North America])

Appendix: Map Reading

Assignment:

You will be looking at a variety of maps. Choose a map from the selection. Open it so it lies flat on the table. Answer the following questions (Some maps may not have all these items. In that case, write: *not applicable* or *NA*):

1. What is the title of this map?_____.
2. Find the *compass rose*. Which way is north? Draw an arrow here that shows which way is north.
3. Does the map have a *key* or *legend?* _____. If so, where is it located?_____.

Write five *symbols* from the key and tell what they mean.

A.

B.

C.

D.

E.

4. Does the map tell any *distances?* _____ Copy the *scale,* if given.

5. Are there nations, countries, or states on your map? _____

   List some of them here:

6. Are there cities on your map? _____

   List some of them here:

7. Select three places that look interesting to you. Write something about them here:

A.

B.

C.

8. What do you like about this map?

   What don't you like?

Contributor

Joan M. Dungey has taught ESL at all levels and is curriculum coordinator at Yellow Springs High School. She also teaches in the languages and literature department at Cedarville College and in the education department at the MacGregor School of Antioch University, in Ohio, in the United States.

Where Is It? Let's Go!

Levels
Intermediate

Aims
Develop map reading
skills and vocabulary
Learn about the
geography of the host
country and city in an
interactive and
enjoyable way
Practice group
discussion and writing
skills

Activity Type
Application

Class Time
1 hour

Preparation Time
30–60 minutes

Resources
City map showing
places of interest
Related tour guides

Students practice language and map-reading skills in this geography activity as they plan to visit a city and enjoy the local attractions. The focus can be related to topics studied in a content class: historical sites, entertainment sites, or sites of economic or political importance.

Procedure

1. Organize students into small groups and explain that they will plan a vacation trip to another city. Distribute a city map and related guides for this activity.

2. Provide the following instructions to the groups (in writing, on the board, an overhead transparency, or a worksheet)

   - As a group, choose a time of year for the visit based on seasonal activities available in the area.
   - Select a hotel from the tour guide, and figure out how much it will cost your group to stay for 4 days.
   - Estimate the cost of meals for 4 days. Use the tour guide to choose restaurants.
   - Select at least two places of interest to visit each day.
   - Decide on the type of transportation needed to get to the sites (e.g., taxi, subway, bus). Estimate transportation costs within the city (e.g., if you are in New York City, what will you pay to travel from your hotel to the World Trade Center?).

3. When the groups finish, have them report to the class on their travel plans and costs.

Caveats and Options

1. One variation is for teachers to prepare guiding questions for the activity, such as the following:

   New York City
   ● What areas represent the economic importance of this city? (Wall Street, garment industry)
   ● Locate Wall Street on the city map.
   ● What international political organization can you visit? (The United Nations)
   ● What do people go to New York to see? (Broadway, Empire State Building)

2. Design the activity so students participate based on their individual abilities. More advanced students can write out the answers and give the reasons they have chosen to visit certain areas of interest, or how certain organizations affect the world scene.

3. Keep the exercises interesting and relevant. Students should be encouraged to invent their own situations; they can constantly rework the given material as they go over it in class.

References and Further Reading

Chamot, A.U., & Kupper, L. (1989). Learning strategies in foreign language instruction. *Foreign Language Annals, 22* (1), 13-24.

Krashen, S., & Terrell, T. (1983). *The natural approach.* Oxford: Pergamon.

Melvin, B., & Stout, D. (1987). Motivating language learners through authentic materials. In W. Rivers (Ed.), *Interactive language teaching* (pp. 44-56). New York: Cambridge University Press.

Taylor, B. (1982). In search of real reality. *TESOL Quarterly, 16,* 29-42.

Contributor

Douglas Magrath teaches ESL and college writing at Embry-Riddle Aeronautical University and Daytona Beach Community College, in Florida, in the United States. He has provided ESL workshops in Florida and presented at local and regional TESOL meetings.

Looking for a Home

Levels
Any; high school
(Grades 11-12)

Aims
Use prepositions of time
and place
Read and interpret a
city apartment guide
Practice forming
questions

Activity Type
Application

Class Time
1 hour

Preparation Time
30 minutes–1 hour

Resources
City apartment guide

In this activity, students examine housing options using an apartment guide to locate, compare, and contrast different apartment complexes as to price, amenities, and convenience. At the same time students practice forming *wh-* questions and using prepositions.

Procedure

1. Pass out copies of an apartment guide to the students.
2. Use the target structures (e.g., prepositions) in explaining the guide and new vocabulary to the students.
3. Begin asking questions about the guide using simple yes/no questions to elicit responses from students at lower proficiency levels. Use questions involving more difficult constructions and concepts for higher proficiency levels.
4. Have students form teams, select a location, and give each other directions to the complex from the school. Then have students role-play an apartment hunter and rental agent. For students who need some guidance, refer to sample questions and answers on Appendices A and B. More proficient students can also role-play inspecting the apartment.
5. Have students decide if they will take the apartment they have been examining. Students participate based on their individual abilities. Less proficient students can explain orally. More advanced students can write out the reasons why they have chosen to take or not take the apartment. Students can also write a letter to a friend telling about their new home.

Caveats and Options

1. Adjust the activities appropriately for mixed proficiency levels in the class.
2. Follow-up activities may include problem solving (e.g., what to do when something breaks down in the apartment), additional reading and writing tasks (e.g., write a letter about moving), computer-assisted instruction (e.g., looking for rentals on-line), and a work station approach where students work alone or in small groups.
3. The more proficient students could create a new apartment guide based on information provided by the teacher.

References and Further Reading

Chamot, A.U., & Kupper, L. (1989). Learning strategies in foreign language instruction. *Foreign Language Annals, 22* (1), 13–24.

Krashen, S., & Terrell, T. (1983). *The natural approach.* Oxford: Pergamon.

Melvin, B., & Stout, D. (1987). Motivating language learners through authentic materials. In W. Rivers (Ed.), *Interactive language teaching* (pp. 44–56). New York: Cambridge University Press.

Taylor, B. (1982). In search of real reality. *TESOL Quarterly, 16,* 29–42.

Appendix A: Sample Questions to Ask During an Apartment Search

Looking for an Apartment

We are looking at the CITY APARTMENT GUIDE. We are going to visit the_____ (fill in name) apartments. Use the map and written descriptions in the guide to ask and answer these questions:

Sample answers are provided for illustration.

1. Where are the_____ apartments? They are on Fourth Street.
2. Is the complex near a shopping center? Yes, it is $\frac{1}{2}$ mile from Fred's Market.
3. Which floor is the vacancy on? The vacant apartment is _____ the first floor.
4. When can we move in ? We can move in _____ July 1.
5. When is the rent due? It is due _____ the first of every month.
6. Is basic cable included? No, it is not included ____ the monthly rent.
7. Is the Alhambra Arms near the interstate highway? Yes, it is three miles _____ I-4.

8. Do they allow roommates? Yes, they allow up to four people ____ each apartment.

Appendix B: Apartment Quest—More Things to Ask

Now form pairs and take turns asking and answering some questions using the CITY APARTMENT GUIDE. One of you can be an apartment hunter, the other a rental agent. (Key vocabulary comes from the printed descriptions in the guide.)

Sample Topics, Questions, and Answers:

1. Washer/Dryer Connections
   Do the apartments have washer and dryer connections? Yes, they do.
2. Swimming pool
   Where is the pool? When is it open? Is there a lifeguard?
3. Club house
   Is there a club house? Does it have a weight room? (and so forth)
4. Basement storage
   Is there extra storage room in the basement? No, I'm sorry there isn't.

Contributor

Douglas Magrath teaches ESL and writing at Embry-Riddle Aeronautical University and Daytona Beach Community College, in Florida, in the United States. He has published in Foreign Language Annals, TESOL Newsletter, *and* Teaching English to Deaf and Second Language Students.

Apartment Shopping

Levels
Intermediate

Aims
Integrate language with math
Read classified ads
Make real-life applications
Practice making choices
Follow directions

Activity Type
Motivation or application

Class Time
50 minutes

Preparation Time
5 minutes

Resources
Newspaper classified advertisement section
Scissors, glue

Students are very interested in spending money. This activity brings reality to the classroom in a dramatic way while using survival reading materials.

Procedure

1. Review family vocabulary words with the class. Then, ask students to describe apartments or houses they have lived in to review housing vocabulary. Let students share as much as they want and as time allows about their homes.
2. Hand out a newspaper to each student and show them how to find the classified ad section from the index on the front page. Review the newspaper's classified ad section, reminding students about abbreviations that are commonly used. Review these as necessary (e.g., *rm., appl., bdrm., w/w, w/d, dep.*).
3. Distribute the handout. (See Appendix A.) Assist students in describing their family or an imaginary family that needs a home.
4. Have students identify their housing needs according to the family size, answering questions like: *How many bedrooms do you need? How many bathrooms do you need? Do you want a separate dining area?*
5. Help students find the apartments to rent section in the classified ads. Ask them to find five ads that might fit their family and fill out a chart for each one. The chart columns can be headed: No. of bdrms, No. of baths, Other things of interest? Utilities included? Appliances included? Deposit required? First/last months' rent required? Cost/month? (See Appendix B.)

Caveats and Options

1. Extend this activity by shopping for furniture in the same way, using store supplement ads, catalogues, or the newspaper classified section for comparison of used furniture prices.
2. Each student does not need to have the same newspaper; collect them over time. For whole-class newspaper subscriptions, contact your local newspaper's Newspaper in Education (NIE) office for discount prices. Most materials are free and often the newspaper can present an NIE workshop for your school's teachers.
3. The International Reading Association (P.O. Box 8139, Newark, DE 19714-8139 USA) has excellent and inexpensive NIE materials.

Appendix A: Sample Questions to Estimate Apartment Needs

How Much Do Things Cost?

In this activity, you will calculate the costs of housing a family. Describe your family or make up an imaginary family.

How many people are in the household?

Who is the head of the household?

Names of other adult(s) and relationship (e.g., grandfather, aunt)?

Children's names and ages?

Appendix B: Sample Questionnaire and Chart

Finding an Apartment

Using the classified ads in the newspaper, find five possible apartments for your family.

Determine your needs by answering these questions:

How many bedrooms do you need?

How many bathrooms do you need?

Do you want a separate dining area?

Look though the classified ads for apartments. Cut out five ads for apartments and paste them on the chart. Then fill out the chart.

Classified ad	No. of bdrms	No. of baths	Other things of interest	Utilities included?	Appliances included?	Deposit required?	First/last months' rent required?	Cost/ month

Decision: Which apartment would you choose and why?

Contributor

Joan M. Dungey has taught ESL at all levels and is curriculum coordinator at Yellow Springs High School. She also teaches in the languages and literature department at Cedarville College and in the education department at the MacGregor School of Antioch University, in Ohio, in the United States.

Backstepping a Career

Levels
Intermediate

Aims
Trace a career plan
Discuss levels of
achievement for a job
Identify expectations of
employers
Learn and practice ways
of using career-related
vocabulary

Activity Type
Motivation

Class Time
30 minutes

Preparation Time
30 minutes

Resources
Pictures of successful
business people
Step chain
Vocabulary list

This activity motivates students to read about and research the qualifications and experience needed for possible future occupations or careers. With guidance and the use of visual organizers, students are able to backstep a career, tracking back the steps in the chain of experience and education required to reach that particular job.

Procedure

1. Prepare a vocabulary list including words such as *occupation, experience, qualifications, course work, counselor, job training, skills, career, career plan, job search,* and other pertinent terms and expressions from any future assigned readings.

2. Display a visual of a series of steps or a "stepchain" (see Appendix). On the top step is a picture of successful business people. Ask students to think about how these people became successful. Did they have to prepare? What kinds of skills did they need? Explain to the students that they will be completing their step series.

3. Ask students to complete the space just under the top step with the job of one of the successful business people in the picture and the place of employment. For example, "manager" or "Jane is a manager. She works for a large supplier of hospital food."

4. Ask how that person got the job. Did this person have an interview? Was he or she an applicant? Did he or she prepare for the interview? Did he or she have to take a test? On the next step down, have students write what their business person did to get the job.

5. Then ask what the individual did to prepare for this job. Did this person have an entry-level job? What was that job? On the next step down, have students write what preparation the person had.

6. Now ask what the person did to get this entry-level job. Was the applicant interviewed? Was there a placement by a college job counselor? Tell students to write what happened on the next step.
7. Next ask where the person was before getting a job. Did the person talk to a counselor about job qualifications for this job? Did the counselor talk about the experience required to become a successful manager? Students should write the answer on the next step down.
8. Now ask where this person was before talking to the counselor about the job. Was this person in school acquiring skills for the job? What courses were most helpful? Have students answer on the next step down.
9. What did this student do before deciding which courses to take? Did this student speak to a school counselor about course work best suited to provide preparation for this kind of career? Tell the students to write this information on the lowest step.
10. Pair the students. Each student will tell the story forward, to his or her partner, starting on the lowest step and working up, one step at a time. The students will talk about the preparation and career path of a successful business person.

Caveats and Options

1. You may want to make an overhead transparency during the initial discussion stage or while students are doing their own step chains. You can display the overhead in order to elicit model responses in a large group.
2. Key vocabulary words can be presented orally first, followed by a written list given to the students for further study. Additional vocabulary activities can be assigned at the end of the lesson.
3. This activity may be used as a motivation and preview to reading a chapter on career choice in an occupational education text.
4. As an application activity, students may be assigned readings about various jobs. They will fill in a step chain using a career they have researched or read about. They can share their findings with the whole class or in pairs. They can write a narrative about a career using their step chains.

5. This activity can be conducted with lower level students by using more basic vocabulary and by having the more able students model the story of the career first in a large group using the overhead. Students with emerging literacy may draw pictures instead of writing in the boxes.

6. Another option is to model this step chain after an adult known to the students, such as a local government figure, a staff person in the school district, or a medical specialist. Students could interview this person.

References and Further Reading

Jameson, J. (1994). *You can help content teachers teach LEP students effectively*. Presentation at the 28th Annual TESOL Convention, Baltimore, MD.

Jones, R. (1989). *Getting ready: Decisions/jobs/careers 1989*. Albany, NY: Delmar.

Short, D. (1991). *How to integrate language and content instruction: A training manual*. Washington, DC: Center for Applied Linguistics.

Tang, G. (1993). Teaching content knowledge and ESOL in the multicultural classroom. *TESOL Journal, 2* (2), 8-12.

Appendix: Sample Step Chains for Backstepping a Career

Backstepping a Career

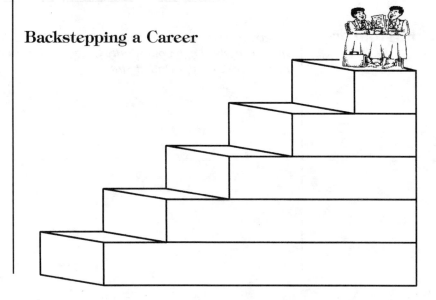

Sample Completed Step Chain for Backstepping a Career

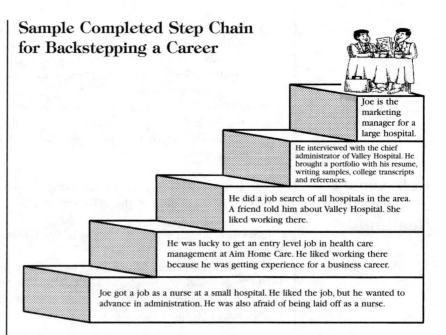

Joe is the marketing manager for a large hospital.

He interviewed with the chief administrator of Valley Hospital. He brought a portfolio with his resume, writing samples, college transcripts and references.

He did a job search of all hospitals in the area. A friend told him about Valley Hospital. She liked working there.

He was lucky to get an entry level job in health care management at Aim Home Care. He liked working there because he was getting experience for a business career.

Joe got a job as a nurse at a small hospital. He liked the job, but he wanted to advance in administration. He was also afraid of being laid off as a nurse.

Contributor

Maxine Endy teaches at Clara Barton High School for Health Professions, Kingsborough Community College, and the College of New Rochelle, in New York, in the United States.

Career Search

This activity encourages students to think seriously about their futures as they explore the school career resource center and its human and material resources. They share their research with the class as they discuss their potential careers.

Procedure

1. Explain the postsecondary educational system to students, using a graphic organizer like a ladder or staircase to indicate the hierarchy of higher education. (See Appendix A.)
2. Review structures such as *must, have to, must not, doesn't/don't have to*. Discuss general occupations and elicit commonly known qualifications, such as "a teacher has to have a bachelor's degree."
3. Bring in a selection of job advertisements from your local newspaper. Include a full range of possible career choices with varying educational requirements.
4. Ask students to select a job to study. Give them a brief worksheet for listing the job, its duties, and its requirements. Assist students with difficult terminology and abbreviations in the ads and have them share their information with a partner.
5. Provide a copy of the GIS index so students can explore a full range of career possibilities as well as a listing of occupations by cluster (e.g., public service, health, transportation). Have the students review the list and check occupations that seem interesting to them. They should choose one to research before going to the Career Resource Center (CRC).
6. Take students on an in-school field trip for an orientation to the CRC. Have the career counselor introduce himself and the resources that are available. (See reference list.) Give students research guidelines, a

scoring rubric (see Appendix B), and time to gather information about their job.

Caveats and Options

1. Students may need more than one class period to research their career. Be sure they know the policy on use of resources, CRC hours, and other information required to work on their own.
2. If the GIS index is not available, use the employment section of the newspaper to create a comprehensive list of jobs.
3. You may adjust the point value for the items on the scoring rubric according to your objectives.

References and Further Reading

Career Briefs. (1993). Career Occupational Preference System. San Diego, CA: ERAS.

Career World [magazine]. Field Publications.

Cosgrove, H.R. (Ed.). (1997). *Encyclopedia of careers and vocational guidance.* (10th ed.) Vols. 1–4. Chicago, IL: J.G. Ferguson.

Guidance Information System [computer program]. (1995). Chicago, IL: The Riverside Publishing Company.

Lidz, R., & Perrin, L. (Eds.). (1996). *Career information center.* (6th ed.) New York: Simon & Schuster Macmillan.

U.S. Department of Labor, Bureau of Labor Statistics. (1996). *Occupational outlook handbook, Bulletin 2470.* (1996–1997 ed.) Washington, DC: U.S. Department of Labor.

Schmidt, P. (1993). *Careers without college.* Princeton, NJ: Petersons.

Appendix A: Sample Graphic Organizer, Steps to Higher Education

+ 4 years — PhD Degree
+ 2 years — Master's Degree
+ 2 years —
+ 4 years — Bachelor's Degree
+ 2 years — Associate Degree
High School Diploma

STEPS TO HIGHER EDUCATION

Appendix B: Sample Guidelines for Oral Presentation Assignment on Careers

1. At the CRC, research a job that you would like in the future or one that you think is interesting.
2. Take notes on responsibilities and qualifications for your job.
3. Include reasons why you think this would be a good job (e.g., interesting work, exciting/adventurous, work with people, make a lot of money)
4. Prepare a 2- to 3-minute oral report on your job.
5. Include the following grammar structures in your presentation: *must, have/has to, must not, don't/doesn't have to.*
6. Make your presentation creative by including pictures, photos, art, music, job equipment, and so forth.

Scoring Rubric (maximum point value indicated)

During the presentation, the student has

____ at least 4 correct uses of expressions of need: *must, have/has to, must not, doesn't/don't have to.* (44)

____ a complete discussion of job duties (12)

____ a complete discussion of job qualifications (8)

____ an explanation of why this would be a good job (8)

____ good introduction (5)

____ good conclusion (5)

____ good eye contact (4)

____ good posture (4)

____ finished within the time limit (5)

____ a creative presentation (5)

Contributor

Carolyn Bohlman teaches secondary ESL in Illinois, in the United States. She has also taught adult education ESL and has been a consultant and teacher trainer.

The Dream Job Interview

Levels
Intermediate +; high
school

Aims
Explore personal talents
Use practical English in
writing and speaking
Think critically

Activity Type
Motivation

Class Time
1 hour

Preparation Time
10–15 minutes

Resources
Sample student resume,
cover letter, and job
advertisement clippings

Caveats and Options

This job interview activity gives students the opportunity to learn ways to promote themselves in English, which may require them to adopt a new cultural perspective. Students find the activity immediately gratifying because they can use these skills in their own part-time or full-time job search.

Procedure

1. Ask each student to clip a classified advertisement of a job they dream of having. If they cannot find an ad for the right job, they can write their own dream job description.
2. For homework or in class, ask students to write a resume and cover letter. It is best to give them one good sample to work from. Help them use active verbs and adjectives that are descriptive and have impact.
3. Discuss the format of a job interview with the class. This is an opportunity to share the cultural appropriateness of the types of questions asked in job interviews. Explain how students might respond to interviewer's questions and suggest that students ask some questions themselves near the end of an interview.
4. Personalize this activity by asking each student to participate in a private job interview of about 10 minutes. Look at the students' job description and put yourself in the interviewer's shoes. Ask different questions depending on the content of the job described.

1. As students prepare their resumes, you can give the students the option to create experiences that they hope to have in the future and to write as though they have already lived through these events (e.g., the high school student might say that he or she has finished college,

or that he or she went to medical school, or has 7 years of teaching experience.)

2. This activity can be adapted for beginners by changing the requirements and making the interview very basic.

3. It may be necessary to help students decode the abbreviations found in the job advertisements.

4. As a result of the interview or as a separate activity, students might wish to work with you or a peer to revise their resumes.

5. Students can evaluate their own performance at the interview, particularly if the students feel intimidated about their spoken English. After all, this exercise is for building confidence and a practical experience. The class might create a self-evaluation form to use. Videotaping or audiotaping the interviews can aid the self-evaluation process.

Contributor

Naoko Tani is an assistant professor at Kwansei Gakuin University in Nishinomiya, Japan. She has an MA in TESOL and an MEd in Counseling Psychology from Teachers College, Columbia University.

Apply to the College of Your Dreams

Levels
Advanced; high school

Aims
Explore personal talents
Use practical English in
writing
Explore U.S. college
application procedures
Think critically

Activity Type
Motivation

Class Time
1 hour

Preparation Time
Variable

Resources
As wide a selection of
competitive school
application essays as
possible
College admissions essay
questions that can be
obtained by writing to
various colleges
Video clip on college
admissions

In this activity, students learn new ways to promote themselves in English, which may require them to adopt a new cultural perspective. By selecting a university they would like to attend, students find out what it takes to be accepted. This may be particularly appropriate in EFL settings, but can be adapted for other settings.

Procedure

1. In class, show students a video of the admissions process at a college in the United States. Discuss the main points in class and compare with the admissions process in the students' home countries. Raise advantages and disadvantages of both processes.
2. Prepare a list of schools for which you have applications. Have each student select a college or university from the list. The more recent the essay questions, the better.
3. As a class, brainstorm points to raise in a sample essay. The expectation that students should promote themselves in some types of admissions essays may be uncommon in some cultures and therefore worth exploring in class.
4. For homework or in class, ask students to write an English essay of about 250 words for the particular university they chose. This is a good opportunity for them to learn to use the word processor.

Caveats and Options

1. For Step 2, you can give the students the option to choose from a list of questions instead of a list of universities, depending on your purpose.

2. This activity can be adapted for the intermediate level by changing the requirements and making the essay very basic.
3. This activity can be extended with a class publication of the students' college admissions essays.
4. Students can individually write to schools of their choice and request an application package.

References and Further Reading

Karras, S. (Development Ed.), & Leonhardt, N.L. (Acquisitions Ed.). (1990). *Focus on American culture*. [Videotape]. Englewood Cliffs, NJ: Prentice Hall Regents.

Contributor

Naoko Tani is an assistant professor at Kwansei Gakuin University in Nishinomiya, Japan. She has an MA in TESOL and an MEd in counseling psychology from Teachers College, Columbia University.

Part IV: Multimedia Infusion

Editor's Note

The activities in this section incorporate technology in the language learning process. A number of the techniques add drama to the mix as students watch videos and television, or listen to audiotapes. Through physical actions, visual stimuli, mime, and other performance techniques, students explore language use and nonverbal communication in a multisensory manner. Most of the activities help students develop listening skills and vocabulary knowledge and apply these to writing and speaking tasks. Several of the activities may be used for review and assessment of language or content objectives.

And The Academy Award Goes To . . .

Levels
Intermediate +

Aims
Be creative
Use practical and
expressive English in
writing and drama
Understand body
language

Activity Type
Motivation

Class Time
Variable

Preparation Time
Variable

Resources
5-minute clip from any
videotape or film that
shows body language
TV/video player

This activity encourages students to enjoy English. It gives them the opportunity to learn new ways to express themselves in English and understand how to use body language while speaking.

Procedure

1. In class, show students a 5-minute video clip, without sound, of the movie of your choice. A good section can be found in the 1946 version of *Arsenic and Old Lace* or in the 1945 film, *Blithe Spirit*. Try to find films that students do not know and are not apt to rent at video stores so that they can be creative. Students must decode the body language in the silent movie clip in order to write a script.
2. Divide students into groups of four or five. Have each group write a script together for the film or video scene they viewed and prepare to perform their scene for the class. Spend one or two class periods writing and rehearsing the scene.
3. On performance day, create and distribute a ballot to have all students vote for the Academy Award winning group. The teacher also must vote. Awards include: Best Actor, Best Actress, and Best Screenplay.

Caveats and Options

1. You can make additional awards such as: Best Supporting Actor, Best Supporting Actress, and so on.
2. This activity can be adapted for beginners. One way is to write a class script and then have groups act out the same script. Another is to have student groups create, practice, and act out a script but not necessarily write it all down.

3. Students may be interested in making costumes and building sets for their scenes. Other awards could then be given.
4. This activity can be followed up with a class publication of the scripts.

Contributor

Naoko Tani, an assistant professor at Kwansei Gakuin University in Nishinomiya, Japan, has more than 5 years EFL experience. She has an MA in TESOL and an MEd in counseling psychology.

Who Killed Mrs. Rosen?

Levels
Intermediate; high
school

Aims
Prepare for persuasive
essay or report writing
through oral practice

Activity Type
Critical thinking and
application

Class Time
40 minutes

Preparation Time
Variable
Making a video can take
as long as $1\frac{1}{2}$ hours.
Choosing a segment
from a commercial
movie may take as long
as $2\frac{1}{2}$ hours if it is
necessary to view the
movie before deciding
what you would like to
use.

Resources
Video camcorder for
preparation
TV/Video player

This activity stimulates persuasive debate and sequential reporting. Because the video characters are persons the students know, they are eager to share their views, which makes conceptualizing the particulars of persuasive essay writing and report writing easier.

Procedure

1. Before this lesson, students should have been taught the basic principles of writing reports and persuasive essays. The lesson may be used as a practical application for reporting a crime or for demonstrating the use of details to support opinions.

2. To prepare, create a video with your colleagues that will be conducive to reporting or debating. Create, for example, a murder scene or a robbery; alternatively, you may use a segment from a movie. The students must decide who committed the crime. (Our video, "Who Killed Mrs. Rosen?", showed interactions between two characters with a woman who was later found dead. In Scene 1, a woman in her home is visited by another woman wearing a scarf who is upset with her about something. They argue. The scene ends. In the next scene, a second woman visits. She arrives with a bowl of grapes. She discovers the same information the first visitor discovered and she is upset. The two argue. In the third scene, grapes are found in the hands of the dead woman and the scarf is nearby. A detective arrives and appears perplexed. On camera, the detective points out the particulars of the case. Either of the characters could have been responsible for the murder, but the students must decide.)

3. Before playing the video, review vocabulary with students (e.g., evidence, motive, commit), and direct students to look for conflicts and to observe details closely.

4. Play the videotape in class. Clarify vocabulary and concepts as needed. At a second viewing, encourage students to take notes.
5. Do one of the following:
   - Use the video to prepare for persuasive writing. After viewing, form student groups to solve the crime. Each group must reach consensus as to who is guilty and must give details to support its opinion. A spokesperson from each group reports the group's opinion.
   - Use the video to prepare for report writing. Form groups to report the crime. One group will report the beginning of the story or crime. This group will answer the *wh-* questions about the crime. Assign an episode of the story to each of the other groups who will report it in sequential order. A spokesperson from each group should report the events.
6. Replay the video to allow students to check details. You may allow time for students to debate differing opinions.
7. The students will then write their own versions of the video, either as a report on the event (as for a newspaper article) or as a persuasive document (as for a defense or prosecuting brief). This can be done the following day in class or for homework. Sharing the students' work provides a delightful, affective element.

Caveats and Options

1. The video we used did not have any dialogue. This was done purposefully to allow other members of the foreign language/ESL department to use it.
2. Use your own group-formation guidelines. We found that four groups of three–five students worked well. Groups may or may not have the same assignment.
3. Using colleagues to create the video will inspire high interest and motivate students to get involved in the lesson. The benefits are numerous, and the project is enjoyable.
4. For less proficient students, use the video to develop reporting skills. After viewing the video several times, have the students relate what happened.
5. In New York, students are required to pass a Regents competency exam in writing. One part of the test is writing a report; another is

writing a persuasive essay. Once the mechanics of writing a persuasive essay and a report have been taught, the use of a video, without words, is a helpful vehicle for discussion and writing.

6. Additional use of the video is endless. It may be used to teach vocabulary, emotions, sequence, descriptions, culture, and values, to name a few ideas.

References and Further Reading

Lonergan, J. (1984). *Video in language teaching.* Cambridge: Cambridge University Press.

Contributors

Karen Rosen and Bonnie Johnson have both taught ESL for more than 10 years at the high school and community college levels in New York, in the United States.

Cartoon Time

Levels
Beginning; middle
school

Aims
Revise and extend
vocabulary
Revise and extend use
of verb tenses
Develop awareness of
the structure of a text
Practice speaking and
writing

Activity Type
Review and application
of skills

Class Time
1 hour

Preparation Time
1 hour

Resources
5-minute videotape of
cartoons
TV/video player

This activity can be used to review or introduce language structures and vocabulary. Simple narrative patterns can be introduced, including the use of dialogue in a text.

Procedure

1. Record a video of popular cartoons choosing those that you know your students like watching or are familiar with.
2. Watch the video and decide what vocabulary students will need to be able to talk about it.
3. Introduce the topic of the lesson (i.e., the theme of the cartoon story) to the students and elicit any information they already know about the cartoon characters. If needed, preteach key vocabulary.
4. Play the videotape for the students without any sound.
5. Ask students what the story was about, what the main events were, and the order in which events happened. Help students with vocabulary and grammar as they summarize the cartoon.
6. Replay the tape, stopping it at suitable points. Ask students to tell you what is happening and help them with any new vocabulary or language structures.
7. After showing the tape for the second time, ask students to retell the story in more detail and make ordered notes on the board.
8. Elicit from students information about the sequence of events in the story.
9. Ask students to write their own story based on the video and using the notes on the board.

Caveats and Options

1. With short cartoons which use only sound effects, play the video with the sound and introduce the sound words to the students.
2. After students have completed their stories, play the videotape with sound for the class.
3. With more advanced students, use a longer cartoon or a cartoon with dialogue and play the tape with sound the second time. This will help more advanced students create a more detailed story.
4. The writing activity can be done as pair work or a small-group activity.
5. Ask students to add to the story and put in their own dialogue.

Contributor

Jackie Wheeler works as a lecturer for the Hong Kong Institute of Education, training teachers and teaching ESL. She has worked at the tertiary and secondary levels.

What Did He Do?

Levels
Beginning-intermediate

Aims
Review use of verb
tenses
Practice speaking and
writing

Activity Type
Review or assessment

Class Time
40-50 minutes

Preparation Time
20-40 minutes

Resources
TV/video player
Mr. Bean video or
appropriate video of
your choice

Using videotape content to generate conversational responses, this activity can be used to review or assess the use of tenses, generally or in different combinations. The action is also intended to stimulate students to communicate with their peers and their teacher.

Procedure

1. Have your chosen videotape ready to show. The *Mr. Bean* series (with actor Rowan Atkinson) is excellent for this purpose, but any video that has clear action and limited dialogue would be appropriate. Decide in advance what verb tense(s) you wish to concentrate on, such as *past simple, past perfect,* or *present continuous.* Tell students they are going to watch a video and that they should notice what the people are doing in it. Explain that what is being said is not important so they do not have to listen too closely, but they have to watch carefully.

2. Play 5–10 minutes of the video. Try to stop at an appropriate stage in the action.

3. Ask students questions about what they have seen. Phrase the questions in a manner that will elicit responses using the predetermined verb tenses. For example, to review past simple past and past continuous, you could ask the following questions: "What was the man doing in the park?" "What did he have in his hand?" "What did he do then?"

4. Encourage students to talk about the video. Promote discussion about the activities of the characters and the students' responses to what they have seen (e.g., "Did you like what he did?" "Was that behavior culturally appropriate?"). Responses to such questions

should be given in the appropriate tense. If they are not, you can restate the students' comments using the correct tense.

5. Show a further 10 minutes of the video and again encourage students to discuss what they have seen. From your previous questions they will probably have picked up the use of the focused tenses and be using them more naturally. If they are not, continue to ask leading questions and to guide the students indirectly.

6. After a suitable period of discussion or when you feel students' attention wandering, change the direction of the activity by handing out a prepared question sheet (see Appendix).

7. Explain the task to the students and give them a set time in which to complete the activity. This task could be done in pairs or individually.

8. While the students are working on the task, monitor their activity. If they are not responding in appropriate tenses, guide them toward the correct tense.

9. At the end of the allotted time, call a halt and either have the students hand in their work, if they have been working individually, or read out what they have written. If time is short and you have been monitoring during the exercise, having students read some of the responses to Question 10 from the list in the Appendix would be more beneficial than reading the answers to all the questions.

Caveats and Options

1. This activity can be adjusted to different levels of proficiency depending on the verb tenses selected.

2. The exercise could also be used to review physical descriptions or character description.

3. Students could be encouraged to write dialogue for the characters in the video.

4. A series of role-plays could be devised from the dialogue written by the students.

5. At higher proficiency levels, the video could be used to promote discussion on social versus antisocial behavior.

References and Further Reading

Atkinson, R., & Curtis, R. (Writers). Davies, J.H., Birkin, J, & Weiland, P. (Directors). The Complete Mr. Bean, Vols. 1 & 2 [Videotapes]. London: Video Collect International. (Available from discount and video stores and some supermarkets; URL www.mrbean.co.uk)

Appendix: Sample Worksheet for *Mr. Bean* videotape

1. Where was Mr. Bean?
2. Was it a nice day?
3. Were there many people in the park?
4. What was Mr. Bean doing?
5. Did Mr. Bean have anything in his hand? If he did, what was it?
6. What did the man do for Mr. Bean?
7. Was this a good thing to do?
8. What did Mr. Bean do to the man?
9. Why was Mr. Bean running around?
10. What happened at the police station? (Write four or five sentences talking about what happened and what people did.)

Contributor

Leanne Wilton is currently with the English Language Unit, University of Wales Aberystwyth, in the United Kingdom. She has taught ESL in secondary schools and language schools in Turkey and Australia.

Video Freeze

Levels
Beginning

Aims
Review vocabulary
Identify people and
their roles
Discuss the local
community

Activity Type
Assessment or review

Class Time
20 minutes

Preparation Time
2-4 hours

Resources
Video camcorder for
preparation
TV/video player

This activity may be used as a quick review or assessment of student knowledge about the local community, including roles of public servants and places of interest. The video brings the local community to life and highlights the community's resources.

Procedure

1. While developing a unit on the community, plan assessment objectives, including the questions you would like students to be able to answer.
2. To prepare for the assessment activity, create a videotape of your local community, using your objectives as a guide. Be sure to tape some action scenes of people such as police officers, firefighters, and school crossing guards. If desired, interview some of these people on camera.
3. Play the videotape in class and question students about what they see. Vary the difficulty of the questions: simple identification, vocabulary review and description questions, comparison questions (e.g., compare the jobs of paramedics and police officers), inferential questions (e.g., what might a community do if it had no fire department?).
4. At different points during the videotape, stop the tape and have one or more students enact a freeze model of the scene, taking the part and physical posture of the characters. Acting as a reporter, you, or another student, may interview the frozen students, asking questions about the job, uniform, intentions, routine activities, and so forth. The frozen students thaw in turn to respond to the questions.

Caveats and Options

1. Before individualized assessment begins, you may want to play the whole videotape for the students. Then replay, stopping at appropriate points and questioning the students.
2. This activity may be done as a writing assessment where students list and describe what they see in the videotape.
3. This activity may be prepared for more advanced levels by changing either the video subject or changing the sophistication of the questions posed.
4. Consider interviewing some of the individuals on videotape to elicit more information about their roles in the community. Some of them might pose questions to the students that could be incorporated into the assessment.
5. You may want students to pose their own questions about the videotape and solicit responses from their classmates.
6. The videotape may also be used for instruction, not only for assessment.
7. If a video camcorder is unavailable, take slide pictures of the scenes and display them using an overhead projector to enlarge the projection.

References and Further Reading

McMahon, M., & Yocum, C. (1994). Video quizzes: An alternative assessment. *Science and Children, 32* (2), 18–20.

Contributor

Deborah Short has taught secondary ESL and EFL in California, New York, Virginia, and Congo (Zaire). She conducts research on integrated language and content instruction at the Center for Applied Linguistics, in Washington, DC, in the United States.

Global Worksheets for Authentic TV Viewing

Levels
Intermediate +

Aims
Watch television in
English with confidence
and enjoyment
Understand and utilize
the information given in
English on television

Activity Type
Critical thinking and
application

Class Time
30 minutes +

Preparation Time
Several hours to tape
and edit TV programs
Several hours to prepare
worksheets

Resources
TV/video player/
recorder
Tape editing machine or
second video recorder

This activity helps students understand and use information provided on local television broadcasts including news, sports, weather, film reviews, and advertisements. The activities are designed to be authentic and to increase students' independence.

Procedure

1. If you want to keep a tape library of local TV broadcasts, write to your local TV stations and ask for copyright permission. If you state that you are keeping only local broadcasts (nothing syndicated) for educational purposes, they should grant permission. (See Appendix A.)
2. Once you have copyright permission, tape the items you want. If you have the time and equipment, edit the segments so that you have a separate tape of news pieces, a tape of weather pieces, and so forth.
3. Copy the worksheets in Appendix B or revise them to your needs and then copy. Each worksheet has pre-, concurrent, and postviewing activities. These can be used with very little modification. However, some of the postviewing activities require some support material such as copies of print advertisements, local maps, and other items. You will need to modify these activities and materials to fit your situation.
4. Give the students the videotape and worksheets to complete independently or integrate them into your lesson plans.
5. Some general instructions for the students:
   - Listen to the video segment as many times as you need to complete the worksheet.
   - Go on to the next question if you do not know the answer. Come back to the missed question later.

- Make guesses or predictions if you are not sure of the language you heard.
6. Some general instructions for the teacher:
   - Do the Before-, While-, and After Viewing activities as a whole class, but allow students to work in small groups to give students support throughout the completion of the worksheets. Have follow-up discussions with the small groups to check student answers and understanding of the tape. Have each group report to the class on one section of the worksheet.
   - Once the worksheets have been completed, get feedback from the students on various aspects of language including: what was difficult, what was easy, how they were able to figure out the answers, how they felt about the activity, and if they noticed any personal strengths or weaknesses.

Caveats and Options

1. If you do not want to develop a videotape library, just tape a local news broadcast and play it back during class time. In this way, you can avoid asking for copyright permission and avoid editing the videotape.
2. Put all the worksheets together in a package. Make the package and the videotapes available to students on a self-study basis. Create a cover page with instructions for the students.
3. Demonstrate how to use the material as a whole-class activity. Use one worksheet or a part of one worksheet and guide the students through the viewing and completion of the assigned activities.
4. Use materials you already have available in your institution for follow-up activities.

References and Further Reading

Lynch, A. (1982, Spring). "Authenticity" in language teaching: Some implications for the design of listening materials. *British Journal of Language Teaching, 21,* 9–15.

Rogers, C.V. (1988). Language with a purpose: Using authentic materials in the foreign language classroom. *Foreign Language Annals, 21,* 467–477.

Appendix A: Sample Format for Obtaining TV Copyright Permission

Information to provide to a local TV station from which you are asking copyright permission:

1. Description of material: for example, locally produced news reports, sports reports, weather reports, current affairs programs or television advertisements
2. Details of proposed presentation: for example, (a) materials would be videotaped, then edited and grouped together under the same topic area (e.g., a news tape, a sports tape, a weather tape); (b) students would watch the edited videotape and be asked to complete various language activities
3. Teaching situation in which material would be used: (describe students and situation)
4. Method of reproduction: for example, programs would be videotaped and then edited by a teacher onto another VHS format tape
5. Rights requested: for example, (a) make videotapes of directly broadcast local programs; (b) edit the material and keep a single edited videotape of each topic area for use solely in (your institution) and under supervision; (c) repeated viewing over the course of a semester
6. Organization requesting permission: (your department, institution, telephone, fax)

Appendix B: Advertisement Global Worksheet

Before Viewing Discussion

1. Think of three advertisements you remember. Why do you remember them?
2. In what ways do advertisements affect our lives?
3. What is the most effective medium for advertising (e.g., magazines, TV, billboards)? Why?

While Viewing

Prediction

Watch the video without sound.

1. What is the advertisement for?
2. Write seven words you think will be used in the video segment.

Check Your Prediction

Watch the advertisement again with sound to check whether your predictions were correct or not.

Answer the following questions (watch the advertisement as many times as you like):

1. What groups of people (age, sex, income level) does the advertisement target?
2. How might the targeted audience benefit by using this product or service?
3. How, and when, should the product, or service, be used?
4. How do you feel when you watch the advertisement?
5. What slogan (catchy phrase) is used to sell the product?
6. Think of some other brands of the same product.

After Viewing

What makes an advertisement successful?

	very important important not important	Comments
The product is identified early in the ad.		
It is easy to remember.		
It tells you where you can buy the product.		
Music complements the advertisement or annoys the viewer?		
Famous people are used in the ad. Name three ads that use celebrities.		

Follow-up Activities

1. Choose an advertisement from the ones available. Imagine that you have bought a product after seeing the advertisement on television. However, it does not do what you thought it would do. Phone the company or write a letter of complaint to the company that manufactured the product.
2. Watch the ad again without sound. Prepare a commentary to go with it. Record your commentary and play it together with the ad.
3. Choose a product or service that you are familiar with. Design visual aids and prepare a script to advertise the product. See if the rest of your group or class is able to identify the product.
4. Many people believe that advertisements portray stereotypes of social roles (e.g., mother, father, teacher, doctor), gender, and cultures. Discuss your thoughts on this with the group, using specific examples if you can.
5. Look at the pictures and texts of several advertisements. Then discuss the relevance of the writing to the image.
6. Gather advertisements for different brands of the same product. Discuss the differences between them. Why would you choose a particular brand?

Appendix C: News Global Worksheet

Before Viewing Prediction

1. List three reasons you watch the news.
2. What emotions (if any) might you feel when watching the news?
3. What kinds of stories are included in the news (e.g., politics, murder)?

While Viewing

Fill in the following table for each story in the news broadcast. Remember, you are listening for general details. Do not worry if you can't understand a lot of the language. Watch the segment as many times as you like.

Type of story: (e.g., politics, murder, suicide, war, sport, entertainment)
Emotion: What emotions would viewers feel? (e.g., anger, sorrow, relief, frustration, surprise)
Number of people: How many people are involved in the story?

Location: Where is the action taking place?
Basic facts: What is the general story?

	Type of story	Emotion	Number of people	Location	Basic facts
Story 1					
Story 2					
Story 3					
Story 4					

Reflection

You probably found some of the stories easier to understand than others. Why? Have you heard, read, or talked about any of the stories before? Did this help your understanding?

Specific Viewing

Choose one of the stories from the broadcast. Watch it as often as you wish and complete the following:

1. What is the topic of the story?
2. Write down as many details as you can.
3. Were there any visual aids (e.g., map, on-site pictures, graphs, statistics)? Did they help in your understanding of the story? What did they illustrate?
4. What happened in the story? Was a problem solved or was there a positive effect?
5. What do you think might happen now?

After Viewing

1. Choose one of the news stories from the tape. Imagine you are a journalist writing a story about the case for a local magazine. Prepare a set of questions you would ask the people involved.
2. Prepare a commentary or short talk to accompany one of the news stories (include your impressions, thoughts, feelings).
3. If this was a foreign story, discuss whether it was interesting or important to you or your area of the world.

Appendix D: Film Review Global Worksheet

Before Viewing Discussion

1. What was the most recent film you saw (on television, video, or cinema: in English or another language)?
2. What was your opinion of the film?
3. Do you usually read film reviews in newspapers or magazines or watch them on TV? Which do you prefer?
4. Do the reviews help you to choose a film? If not, how do you decide which films to see?
5. Look at one of the local newspapers to check what is showing at the cinema. Use one or more of the expressions below to describe the types of films showing. If you are unsure of the meaning use a dictionary.

spoof	*science fiction*	*classic*	*love story*
western	*action/adventure*	*documentary*	*comedy*
weepie	*mystery*	*flop*	*tear-jerker*

While Viewing

1. Watch the film review segment of the news as many times as you like.
2. What type of film is being reviewed?
3. Did the reviewer like or dislike the film? Write down some of the language used by the reviewer about the film.

After Viewing

Based on this review or anything else you know about the film, would you like to see it? Give three reasons why or why not.

Follow-up Activities

1. Choose a film through one of the following methods:
   - Refer to the film guide or newspapers provided to choose a film to see this weekend. Each person in the group should give reasons for their choice; or
   - Look at the selection of film videos available and decide on a film to watch.

2. Imagine you are a film critic and do one of the following:
   - Write a review for a magazine of any film you have seen, including information about: the story; the costumes; the acting; and the photography; or
   - Write a review for TV. You may like to videotape yourself giving the review.

3. Imagine you are going to interview a famous actor. Write six questions you want to ask the actor and then role-play the interview.

Appendix E: Sports Global Worksheet

Before Viewing Discussion

Do you think well-known sports people should make as much money as they do?

Write down your ideas and discuss with the rest of your group.

Fill in the following table. Discuss your choices with your group members.

Sports I am interested in	Name of team/person and sport they play	Reason I follow them
Local sports team		
Local sports individual		
Foreign sports team		
Foreign sports individual		

While Viewing

Watch the sports segment as many times as you like. Complete the following table:

	Sport	Name	Country	Win/Lose
Individual				
Team				
Location				

Sometimes sports stories are about the personal or professional activities of a player or owner of a team. Was such a story included? If so, what were the details of the story?

After Viewing

1. Some people are more interested in sports stories than news stories. Discuss why.
2. Imagine you have been asked to plan a 45-minute running race. Look at a local map and decide on a route. Draw a simple map for people to follow.

Appendix F: Weather Report Global Worksheet

Before Viewing Discussion

1. Describe the weather today.
2. What do you think the weather will be like tomorrow?

3. Match the weather conditions with the pictures.

showers	sunny	sunny spells
overcast	cloudy	thunderstorms

4. The weather in this area is quite variable. Group the months into seasons and choose adjectives from the box below to describe the weather conditions during these seasons.

hot	humid	overcast	foggy	dry
cool	rainy	blustery	sweaty	wet
close		cloudy		freezing

While Viewing

Part A: Local Weather
Watch the weather segment as many times as you like. Complete the following table.

Today's forecast

| Temperature | | Weather |
high	low	Condition

Tomorrow's forecast

| Temperature | | Weather |
high	low	Condition

Part B: Nonlocal Weather

1. Imagine you are a business person who must regularly go abroad. You will soon be traveling on a business trip. You need to know what the weather will be at your destination.
2. Watch the weather report segment again.
3. You will be traveling to one city in the parts of the world described in the weather report. Choose three cities and complete the following table.

City	Temp - High	Temp - Low	Conditions
a)			
b)			
c)			

4. Based on the weather forecast, discuss with your group members what sort of clothing you would take.

After Viewing

1. Imagine that friends or relatives from overseas are staying with you. Based on the forecast for today and tomorrow, what suggestions will you make for things to do?
2. A friend, relative, or business client is planning to visit you. They write to you before their arrival asking for advice about what kind of clothes to bring, what kind of food is popular, and what activities people do in their free time. Each person in the group must respond (orally or in writing) according to a different time of year. You may find the phrases below useful.

It's very hot in _____.

It's quite humid in _____.

It tends to rain a lot in _____.

It's rather changeable in _____.

It's usually quite sunny in _____.

Contributors

Christine Heuring, a lecturer at Hong Kong Polytechnic University, has an MA in TESL and is interested in independent learning and authentic materials. Sue Fitzgerald is a lecturer at Hong Kong Polytechnic University. She has an MEd in Educational Technology/TESL.

Who Goes There?

Levels
Intermediate +

Aims
Work cooperatively
Write a coherent
narrative

Activity Type
Motivation or
application

Class Time
45–90 minutes

Preparation Time
1–2 hours

Resources
Audiotape recorder

This activity allows students to cultivate creativity and imagination as they hypothesize a scenario and plot that incorporate a series of audiotaped sounds. The audiotape presents a mystery-like context, engaging students in the production of an extended narrative.

Procedure

1. Record a variety of familiar and not-so-familiar sounds on audiotape. A selection of 5–10 sounds might include running water, footsteps, a hair dryer, the pop from opening a can of soda, Velcro flaps separating, a kiss, birds singing, and waves crashing on a beach.

2. Play the audiotape and have students guess the source of each sound. You may or may not confirm their guesses. You may wish to have students brainstorm a list of likely scenarios (e.g., a robbery, a day at the beach, a train station) and characters (e.g., a victim, an old woman, a doctor) that incorporate the audiotaped sounds.

3. Arrange students in groups of four. Groups may be homogeneous or heterogeneous in proficiency level. Instruct each group to write a story with events that incorporate the sounds on the audiotape.

4. Assign one of the following roles to each student: facilitator, encourager, scribe, and timer. The facilitator moves the group through the process of creating a story that incorporates the chosen sounds and contains a beginning, middle, and end. The encourager elicits contributions from each group member. The scribe records the narrative as it unfolds, and the timer focuses the group to complete the task in the allotted time. Allow 20–30 minutes for the writing process, depending on the number of sounds to be incorporated and the complexity of the task (see Option 1).

5. After each group has composed its story, have the groups share their stories with the whole class.

Caveats and Options

1. You may adjust the complexity of the creative task by selecting common or uncommon sounds, and by selecting a single locale (either ordinary or unusual), or a variety of locales (e.g., a house, a train station, and a circus) from which to record a series of sounds.

2. You may require students to incorporate all or some of the sounds in their stories, and to incorporate the sounds in any sequence, or in the sequence of presentation on the audiotape.

3. Less proficient students can write a shorter narrative that incorporates fewer sounds. They may also limit their narrative to a literal description of the sounds, such as, "The phone rang. The door closed."

4. The sounds presented on the audiotape can prompt a variety of texts: a story, short play, dialogue, poem, TV sitcom, or product advertisement. Any of these texts can be presented in a theatrical setting.

5. This activity can be used to motivate a reading lesson by presenting sounds associated with the content of the text; to review or develop new vocabulary by presenting relevant sounds on the audiotape; and to review or introduce a verb tense by presenting sounds in an appropriate context, such as, "Sounds of Marco's Ideal Vacation" (future); "Sounds of People at Work" (present progressive); "A Day in the Life of Julia" (present or past).

6. A set of pictures or objects may be used in place of, or in conjunction with, the audiotaped sounds.

7. Before the groups share their stories with the class, they might revise them for clarity of expression and narrative structure. You may utilize peer revision so that students in each group work cooperatively to revise another group's story. Grammatical accuracy need not be a concern at this stage, unless the activity is being used to review a specific grammatical structure.

**References
and Further
Reading**

McGroarty, M. (1993). Cooperative learning and second language acquisition. In D. Holt (Ed.), *Cooperative learning: A response to linguistic and cultural diversity,* (pp. 19–46). McHenry, IL: Delta Systems/Center for Applied Linguistics.

Contributor

Albert E. Mussad has experience in ESL teaching, curriculum and program development. He is the supervisor of world languages and creative arts for Bound Brook, New Jersey public schools, in the United States.

Part V: Cooperative Projects

Editor's Note

The project orientation of the activities in this section exemplifies an effective way to help students combine their language skills. Most of the activities included here require several class periods to complete and involve the entire class in the creation of the product (e.g., book, library, play). Three of the activities are also designed to pair an ESL class with a regular English language arts class in ways that capitalize on each class's strengths and promote cross-cultural awareness.

LORE, A Classroom Library Program: Part 1, Setting Up

Levels
Any; high school

Aims
Establish a classroom library
Develop previewing, skimming, and categorizing skills

Activity Type
Motivation

Class Time
One–two class periods

Preparation Time
Variable

Resources
Age-, content-, and level-appropriate authentic literature of all kinds in English or students' first languages
Accessible area of the classroom to house the books

The LORE (Love of Reading in English) program can become an important, continuous, and motivational component of the ESL class. As students discover, select, and read materials of real interest, they will develop a love of reading that will enhance their literacy and their lives. The LORE program is described in three parts: setting up a classroom library; reading; and assessing, monitoring, and incorporating language skills into the program.

Procedure

1. Discuss your personal feelings about reading. Describe the pleasures and values of reading as you see them and as they relate to language proficiency. Ask the students how they feel about reading. Tell students that you want them to discover how enjoyable reading can be, and that to do that, the class will create its own library.
2. Collecting books for a classroom library is a continuing part of the activity. Bring in (and have students bring in) no-cost, used reading materials from various places, including home, other teachers and students, and community charitable organizations. To reach students of very low English proficiency, and to validate students' own cultures, include first language materials.
3. As materials are collected, briefly assess each book for acceptability and remove material that is obviously inappropriate. Initial elimination of obviously inappropriate materials requires about 30 seconds per book. Place books that have been initially screened in the designated classroom area.
4. Several times during this collection period, invite students to explore the emerging library for a few minutes at the start and end of class or during other unstructured time. Encourage students to be aware of

the new use of this classroom space and to be interested in book acquisitions to foster class feelings of accomplishment, ownership, and responsibility for the library.

5. Once you have enough books (at least a dozen per student), ask students how they would like to use the books. Record their suggestions as well as your own on an overhead transparency, blackboard, or newsprint. To incorporate reading strategies and all language skills into the program, guide the class toward including major components of the LORE outline (see Appendix A), although significant preferences (yours and your students') in a particular class should be recognized and accommodated.

6. Ask students to each pick out a book and allow them 10 minutes to do so. It will become clear that the library must be organized in some fashion in order to be easily used. Discuss different ways to arrange books (e.g., by size? by color? alphabetically by title? by author? by subject?) and the advantages and disadvantages to each. Ask students what they looked for when they tried to find a book. Most will say that they looked for something "interesting," and that they were interested in different subjects. Use that information to help students organize the library by theme.

7. Have students predict what themes the books will cover, and write these on the board or overhead. Have each student (or pairs) gather a stack of books to sort into themes. Clear enough floor space for them to sort through their stack. Most students will be able to determine themes by examining illustrations and book cover summaries. If themes they had not predicted are found, add them to the list (Appendix B). Once the list seems complete for your collection, write it across the blackboard and have students stack their sorted books on the floor below each theme label. Have a student copy each theme label across the top of a file folder. Have students arrange books into the designated area alphabetically by theme, with labeled file folders separating themes.

8. Keep track of books by using a file box with an index card for each book checked out (Appendix C). Fine damages or losses accordingly, with funds going toward book tape or replacement books. Students

enjoy being "librarian"; you may rotate librarian duties or you may choose to have students earn the right to play the role.

Caveats and Options

1. Be sure to choose books of real interest to the students.
2. Other ways to collect books include holding a bake sale to raise money to purchase new titles or used books; holding a school- or communitywide used book drive; publicizing your needs in school or local papers and professional newsletters; and canvassing religious groups, charitable organizations, and retail outlets.
3. Extra effort may be needed to obtain books that appeal to young male readers, as many are written from the female perspective. You may be surprised at the number of dull, poorly written, or vulgar books on the market for young people. Delete these books from your collection or put them aside for later use in teaching critical reading. At the beginning of the program, try to expose students only to good, high quality books.
4. Elicit the help of capable parents, coworkers, or community members to assess native language materials that have been collected.
5. While categorizing books, students use selective reading, skimming, and predicting from visual cues. Let students discover and use these reading strategies informally at this point, and guide them without directly teaching the strategies.
6. A transformation from book haters to book lovers mysteriously takes place when students feel that the library is truly theirs and that they are free to choose from it. The key word is patience. The most confirmed book haters may take several months and many different attempts at various types of reading before they begin to enjoy it.

References and Further Reading

Routman, R. (1994). *Invitations.* Portsmouth, NH: Heinemann.

Appendix A: Outline for Lore Program

Using Our Classroom Library

I. Choose a book to read
    A. Discuss how we choose the right book
    B. Organize library books alphabetically by theme
II. Read
    A. Apply reading strategies to what we read:
        1. prereading strategies
        2. decoding skills
        3. using context and prior knowledge to understand a passage which may have words we do not know
    B. Help each other with our reading:
        1. ask questions of each other or the teacher
        2. talk to others who have read the same book before
        3. pair up, with one student reading aloud to another
    C. Think about what we read and ask ourselves questions about it (self-monitoring)
III. Write about our reading
    A. Keep reading logs of what and how much we read
    B. Write our thoughts about what we read in our literature response journals
IV. Discuss what we read in small literature discussion groups

Appendix B: Sample Themes in a LORE Library

Adventure
Animals
Biographies
Fantasy
Growing Up (a broad theme, covering many hard-to-classify books)
History (historical biographies could fit here)

Horror
Humor and Games
Picture Books (an important section initially for beginning ESL students)
Science Fiction

Appendix C : Sample Format for Book-Tracking Cards in File Box

(TITLE)	(AUTHOR)	(THEME)
(Student name)	(checkout date)	(book condition at checkout)
(return date)	(book condition at return)	(Fines, if any)

Contributor

Therese Gauthier teaches French and ESL at Langley High School, in Virginia, in the United States. Lorraine Valdez Pierce at George Mason University inspired her to create LORE.

LORE, A Classroom Library Program: Part 2, Reading

Levels
Any; high school

Aims
Be motivated to read
and write
Relate personally to
reading
Share reactions with
others

Activity Type
Practice or application

Class Time
20–40 minutes, at least
once a week.

Preparation Time
1 hour

Resources
Transparency of a
reading excerpt
Overhead projector
The LORE library
Handouts for reading
strategies

The LORE (Love of Reading in English) program can become an important, continuous, and motivational component of the ESL class. As students discover, select, and read materials of real interest, they will develop a love of reading that will enhance their literacy and their lives. The LORE program is described in three parts: setting up a classroom library; reading; and assessing, monitoring, and incorporating language skills into the program.

Procedure

1. After enough books have been collected, encourage students to become familiar with the library. Support their personal involvement with the books by informally discussing what subjects interest them, books they might like to read, books in their native language and with which they are already familiar, and so forth.
2. Ask each student to choose a book to read.
3. Engage the whole class in a prereading activity. Explain what they are doing and why, so that they understand the value of the activity. Have them examine their book covers and tell each other or write down one or two things they think the book will be about. Prompt students to think about their own experiences and how they might relate to their readings.
4. Briefly discuss plot structure at this point, telling students that if they anticipate basic plot components, the books will be easier to read. Discuss, for instance, the typical plot structure of a mystery or a biography. Remind students of the kind of information they will likely find as they begin to read the "setting." Have them write this down (see Appendix A) or record their thoughts on a transparency or blackboard during class discussion.

5. Before anyone gets discouraged by limited reading skills, directly teach and model some key reading strategies. Hand out or post copies of step-by-step "meaning from context" instructions (see Appendix B) and refer to them often. Frequently discuss and model such skills as guessing and decoding, either individually with students' own selections or with the class.

6. Before class, copy a page from a level-appropriate book onto a transparency and highlight words students may not know. In class, explain what the excerpt is about, and prompt students to relate their prior knowledge to it. Record student-generated vocabulary and ideas in a semantic map on the board. Then display the transparency, read it aloud, and (referring to handouts of Appendix B) model each step of the decoding process on highlighted words until students can join in with you or can use the process successfully themselves.

7. Schedule regular class times for sustained silent reading. Tell students that they are expected to read for a certain uninterrupted period of time every day either in or outside of class. You may inform parents of the new program, its goals, and expectations (see Appendix C).

Caveats and Options

1. Especially at first, students may need help in finding level-appropriate material. The optimum level of difficulty to allow for both reading enjoyment and language learning is a book with only about 10 % unknown vocabulary.

2. Sustained silent reading time will vary due to class length and students' level.

3. Asking students to predict story line and plot helps them personalize their reading and establishes a purpose to the reading.

4. Repeat direct teaching of reading strategies frequently throughout the first few months of the program until students have begun using them naturally without prompting.

5. Enlist the aid of parents or other qualified individuals to translate the parent letter into the students' native language(s).

6. The book collection process for the library can continue during this reading activity and beyond.

References and Further Reading

Routman, R. (1994). *Invitations.* Portsmouth, NH: Heinemann.

Appendix A: Sample Prereading Questions

Before I start to read I ask myself:

- Why did I pick this book?
- What do I think it will be about, and why?
- What do I already know about this topic?

I know the book will probably follow this pattern: _____

_____.

I know what to expect from the beginning or "setting" part of my book:

_____.

Appendix B: Sample Strategies for Decoding Vocabulary

What to do when you don't know a word:

1. Look at the word again: the ending, middle, beginning.
2. Think about what kind of word it is: noun? verb? adjective?
3. See if any part of it looks like a word you already know.
4. Read to the end of the sentence, then try the word again.
5. Think about what would make sense.
6. Substitute a word that makes sense.
7. Skip the word and go on.

Appendix C: Sample Letter to Parents

Dear Parent(s),

The LORE (Love of Reading in English) program that we are beginning is an important part of your child's English learning program. Consistent daily reading will improve your child's fluency, vocabulary, comprehension, and writing. Our main goal is for students to find good books that they are interested in reading, because in that way they will discover how enjoyable reading is and choose to make reading (and therefore learning!) a part of their lives.

Our classroom library now has enough materials to allow all students to find something they enjoy. Your child may also find books for the LORE program at home or in other libraries.

Your child will read the LORE books at home as well as in class. Students and I will frequently discuss what has been read independently. Your child will keep a record of daily reading. Your child's responsibility is to read 20–30 minutes each day. You may want to help your child find a quiet time and place for regular reading.

Your child must bring the LORE book to class. All students are expected to take care of their LORE books. They will be fined for lost or severely damaged books.

Please join with me in creating an environment where students will enjoy books for a lifetime. We'll be opening up the world to them.

Thank you for your help, support, and cooperation.

Sincerely,

Please sign to indicate that you have read this letter and return it to me.

Contributor

Therese Gauthier teaches French and ESL at Langley High School in Virginia, in the United States. She was inspired to create LORE by Lorraine Valdez Pierce, at George Mason University.

LORE, A Classroom Library Program: Part 3, Reading Response

Levels
Any; high school

Aims
Read and relate
personally to reading
and share reactions with
others
Keep reading logs and
write in journals
Monitor and assess
reading

Activity Type
Application or
assessment

Class Time
Variable

Preparation Time
Variable

Resources
The LORE library
Copies of "Thinking
About My Reading"
questions for students
and teacher
Student assessment
checklists

The LORE (Love of Reading in English) program can become an important, continuous, and motivational component of the ESL class. As students discover, select, and read materials of real interest, they will develop a love of reading that will enhance their literacy and their lives. The LORE program is described in three parts: setting up a classroom library; reading; and assessing, monitoring, and incorporating language skills into the program.

Procedure

1. Explain that people who love to read often have strong feelings toward books and stories and that one way for students to become aware of such feelings is to keep a journal in which they write their thoughts and reactions as they read. Demonstrate the writing process on an overhead or blackboard, modeling journal entries about your own reading. Allow students to hear, observe, and inquire about your thought processes, experiments, and revisions. Distribute a list of questions (see Appendix A) to which students may refer for journal ideas.

2. Schedule sustained silent reading (SSR) time regularly every week or class period. Vary amount of SSR time according to students' reading levels. Have students keep a reading log (see Appendix B) to record what, how much, and how often they read. Verify, monitor, and assess that information by conducting quick visual checks during SSR.

3. Track students' reading levels by photocopying a page from their most recent books as they finish reading. Date and keep these pages in separate folders or have students staple them into their reading

response journals. Reading the student journals usually takes several minutes per journal.

4. Meet with individual students for brief conferences during SSR for 5-10 minutes per student. Have students bring their book, reading response journal, and reading log to the conference. Ask the students what they think about their books. Choose a question or two from the list of "Thinking About My Reading" questions, or ask the student to share and comment upon a favorite journal entry about that book. Keep anecdotal records of student responses to help you encourage students' efforts and guide them toward appropriate selections.

5. During conferences, note each student's reading comprehension level and use of reading strategies on a simple checklist (see Appendix C). Assess reading comprehension by having students retell a part of their book or answer comprehension questions about their book. Assess reading strategy use by having students read a new section of their book to you and "think aloud" through any reading strategy used. Other assessments can be performed during SSR.

6. Form literature discussion groups of three or four people, in which students conduct interviews about books, recommend books to each other, predict story endings, or share and react to selected passages from each other's reading response journals. Clearly state goals for this activity (e.g., oral communication, critical thinking about reading, learning how others read and perceive what they read) so that students know what you expect. Schedule a regular reading group time, so students can prepare. This group can meet once a week, or once a month, for 20 minutes or more, according to level and group. Monitor groups at random, using anecdotal records to assess oral skills or participation. Share any pertinent observations or notes with individual students during their conferences.

Caveats and Options

1. Explain that the reading log will not be graded and that students will not be compared to one another regarding how much they are able to read. Let students know that the log will be used to assist you in keeping track of how much and what kinds of reading they are doing so that you may guide them toward appropriate reading

selections in the future and determine whether or not they are having a problem with a particular book.

2. Most students will need structure and guidance in the journal writing activity, as the kind of writing and reflection desired is likely to be something they have never been asked to do before.

3. Assure students that the journals are not meant to please you, but to help them relate to and appreciate their reading in a personal way. Have students fold over or otherwise mark journal pages that they do not want to share with you. Assess journals for having a minimum number of entries, but do not grade entries. You may write comments or start a dialogue in the journals instead of assigning grades, but be aware that this can be very time-intensive.

4. Join in literature discussion groups when appropriate, especially if a group needs guidance. Make student interaction as informal as desired, but remember that students generally do better with a great deal of structure at first.

5. Following basic principles of cooperative learning, assign leadership roles within groups. Once students feel comfortable with the routine and know their roles, you will spend less time monitoring groups and more time in the individual student conferences.

References and Further Reading

Routman, R. (1994). *Invitations*. Portsmouth, NH: Heinemann.

Appendix A: Thinking About My Reading

While I'm reading, I ask myself, "Do I understand this? Is the reading too hard or too easy for me?" I enjoy reading because it makes me think. It lets me imagine things I never thought of before. I get to know people (characters) and situations (plots) that are new and interesting. Through reading, I sometimes also learn things about myself.

Other questions to ask myself while I'm reading are

1. Do I like this book? Why or why not?
2. How do I feel about the way this book is written? Why?

3. How is the main character like me or different from me?

4. Does the main character remind me of anyone I know? Why?

5. Does the story seem real? Could it really happen? Why or why not?

6. Would I act the same way the main character does? Why or why not?

7. If I could change the book, how would I change it?

8. Would I like to meet one of the characters? Which one and why?

9. What would I say to a character in the story if I could? Why?

10. How would the story change if it happened in another time or place?

11. What character plays a small but important role in the story? Why is this character necessary to the story?

12. What does the author do to make me want to keep reading?

13. Does the story create a certain mood or feeling? How?

14. Do I have any strong feelings as I read the story? What are they?

15. How are the characters similar to those in other stories I've read?

16. Is there anything that makes this author's work unique? What?

17. What would I like to say to the author if I could speak to him?

There are other questions and thoughts that occur to me as I read, and I can write about some of them in my reading response journal.

Appendix B: Sample Reading Logs

Students' reading logs can be kept in a section of their journals and look like this:

Reading Log

Date	Title	Page where I stopped reading (if end of book, write *Finished*)
_____	_____	_____
_____	_____	_____
_____	_____	_____

Appendix C: Sample Checklist

Individual student checklist for assessment of reading comprehension and use of reading strategies:

Side one   (Student Name)

Date	Reading Strategy	Performed Independently	Performed with Assistance	Not Used

Side two

Date	Comprehension	Retells Story Independently	Retells Story with Assistance	Unable to Retell

Contributor

Therese Gauthier teaches French and ESL at Langley High School, in Virginia, in the United States. Lorraine Valdez Pierce, at George Mason University, inspired her to create LORE.

Second Language Learners and Literature

Levels
Beginning-intermediate

Aims
Become familiar with
literature and authors
Practice a peer evaluation
process
Experiment with
language
Sharpen summarizing
skills (for regular or
honors English students)

Activity Type
Cooperative project

Class Time
ESL class: 9-10 class
periods
Regular or honors
English class: usual time
for class reading of a
novel plus three-four
class periods

Preparation Time
30-60 minutes

Resources
TV/video player
Video version of novel
Computers for word
processing

This cooperative activity between an ESL class and a regular English class exposes second language learners to classic literature read by regular English classes. Regular English students benefit by sharpening their summarizing skills while increasing their awareness of the frustration encountered by second language learners.

Procedure

1. Plan with the regular or honors English teacher to select a novel that both classes can work with (we used *To Kill a Mockingbird* by Harper Lee, 1960). Develop evaluation criteria ESL students will use to review the regular or honors English students' booklets. Devise booklet evaluation sheet.
2. Have the regular or honors English teacher divide the class into groups to write and illustrate a booklet summarizing the novel in fewer than 50 words per chapter with a cover and illustrations.
3. Prepare a background discussion lesson for ESL class: Familiarize the ESL students with relevant features of the novel including background information, historical significance (if any), and characters.
4. Show the ESL class a video or movie of the novel and point out any deviations from the original.
5. Distribute the booklets from regular or honors English class among groups of ESL students. Rotate the booklets among the groups (perhaps 10 minutes per booklet) so all groups can see the variety. Then assign one booklet per group to evaluate.
6. Have ESL student groups prepare a written evaluation of the booklets according to evaluation criteria. (See sample in Appendix A.)
7. Have ESL groups prepare a final written critique on the computer.

8. Have the ESL groups present their booklets and evaluations to the ESL class.
9. Return booklets and evaluations to the regular English class. Encourage the regular or honors English students to discuss the evaluations in their groups and generate ideas for improving communication for future projects.

Caveats and Options

1. Illustrations and cover may be drawn by the ESL students with captions written by the regular English students, in which case each class could evaluate the other.
2. Establish criteria for special features to be included in the booklets to maintain a degree of uniformity. *To Kill a Mockingbird* features included a glossary of "Southern" terms; an introduction of characters; a foreword with a history of Southern culture and a conclusion summarizing the meaning of the story.
3. The size and shape of booklets may be set by the teachers or left to artistic license.
4. Novels to be read at the middle school level might consist mostly of illustrations with captions.
5. Possible authors and books for this cooperative activity are listed in Appendix B.

References and Further Reading

Lee, H. (1960). *To kill a mockingbird.* New York: Harper Collins.
Sharp, J. (1994). Cooperative learning with Honors. *TESOL Journal, 4* (2), 38–39.

Appendix A: Sample Evaluation Sheet

H.P. & M.C.
Per. 2, Beginning ESL
March 13

Evaluation Sheet

We read the booklet "To Kill a Mockingbird" summarized by K.M., E.T., J.L., B.O., and L.D. We enjoyed reading this booklet very much. We evaluate the booklet as follows:

1. Overall Appearance: We thought this book was nice to look at. We did not understand why there was no picture on the cover.
2. Language: We felt that the language of this booklet was just at the right level for us. We understood most of the story as it was written here.
3. Features: We really liked the list of the main characters at the front of the book and the Glossary of Southern terms at the end of the book. These were helpful to us.
4. Illustrations: We thought that the pictures were simple and childish. We thought that we could have drawn more beautiful pictures. We would have used colors in the pictures.

Thank you for involving our class in this project. We enjoyed doing it and reading this story.

Appendix B: Sample Book Lists

Books I would share with high school ESL students:

Steinbeck, J. (1993). *The grapes of wrath.* New York: Harper Collins.
Buck, P. (1995). *The good Earth.* New York: Knopf.
Cormier, R. (1991). *The chocolate war.* Cutchogue: Buccaneer Books.
L'Engle, M. (1984). *A house like a lotus.* New York: Farrar, Straus & Giroux.
Miklowitz, G. (1986). *The war between the classes.* Friday Harbor, WA: Turtleback.
Hunt, I. (1990). *Across five Aprils.* Friday Harbor, WA: Turtleback.
Golding, W. (1959). *Lord of the flies.* Friday Harbor, WA: Turtleback.
Neufeld, J. (1968). *Edgar Allen.* Chatham, NY: S.G. Phillips.
Salinger, J.D. (1951) *The catcher in the rye.* New York: Little Brown.

Books I would share with middle school ESL students:

Steinbeck, J. (1993). *The red pony.* Friday Harbor, WA: Turtleback.
Collier, J.C. (1984). *My brother Sam is dead.* New York: Simon & Schuster.
Mowatt, F. (1956). *Lost in the barrens.* New York: Little, Brown.
Peck, R.N. (1987). *Soup.* New York: Random Library.
Babbitt, N. (1969). *The search for delicious.* New York: Farrar, Straus & Giroux.
Kerr, J. (1997). *When Hitler stole pink rabbit.* Friday Harbor, WA: Turtleback.
Oneal, Z. (1990). *The language of goldfish.* Friday Harbor, WA: Turtleback.

Contributor

Judith Sharp has worked with ESL students since 1980, as librarian at Nishimachi International School in Tokyo, Japan, and as an ESL teacher at South Pasadena High School, in California, in the United States.

Folktale Collection of the World

Levels
Beginning-intermediate

Aims
Compile a multicultural book of folktales from students' native countries
Become familiar with folklore of own countries and classmates' countries
Practice translating from native language to English
Develop editing skills
Develop skills in sentence construction, vocabulary, and spelling
Format table of contents, title page, and book cover

Activity Type
Cooperative project

Class Time
ESL Class: four-five class periods
Regular English class: two class periods

Preparation Time
30 minutes +

Resources
Libraries and family members to help with folktales
Writing lab or computers
Proofreaders for native language stories

This cooperative project between an ESL class and a regular English class familiarizes ESL students with tales from other cultures represented in their classroom and offers an exercise in translation. Students in regular English class practice their editing skills beyond the usual spelling checks, in areas such as combining sentences, altering vocabulary for clarification, and more.

Procedure

1. Ask each student to research a folktale from his or her culture, gathering information from sources such as families, neighbors, and libraries, in preparation for making a class book.
2. Divide students into language groups (where possible) and ask them to collaborate on writing a chosen folktale in their native languages.
3. Collect the folktales and ask native speakers to proofread them.
4. Ask the groups to translate each of the stories into English with support from peer editors. (These may be the group members.) The editors may be of the same language background, but it is not required.
5. Have the groups illustrate their stories with captions in the original language and English.
6. Have students enter the stories on the computer, using a word processing program.
7. Send original language and English versions to a regular English class, which should be divided into groups to edit each story. Each group will revise and edit the English version of one of the stories, leaving the original meaning and story intact. Native language versions of each story are available for reference.
8. Return the edited versions of the stories to the ESL groups who review and discuss changes.

272

9. Have ESL groups type the final copy in English and the original language on the computer. Stories in languages using non-Roman alphabets can be copied in ink if software programs with those fonts are unavailable.

10. To make the class book, ask ESL students to draw and vote for a cover illustration, format a title page and a table of contents, and design the layout of the book and the order in which the stories will appear.

Caveats and Options

1. This activity could work well with middle school students who could prepare a collection for elementary students using mostly illustrations and captions.

2. Some of the initial writing of the folktales could be done as homework.

3. Difficulties could arise with a rare or unfamiliar language; fortunately, we had cooperative parents for proofreading native language versions.

4. The final steps for completing the book could be done with small groups of students taking on different assignments: designing the cover, making the title page, organizing the entries, writing the table of contents, and so on.

5. The regular English students seemed to feel freer to revise work that was not written by themselves or their classmates. This outside perspective aided them in the editing process.

6. Two or three individuals who speak different languages can work together on translations.

7. I was so impressed with the outcome of our book that I color copied all the original language and English stories, the illustrations, the cover, the title page, and the table of contents and bound them. The finished product was exhibited at Back to School Night and several parents offered to finance a personal copy. Copies were placed in the library, the ESL room, and at the District Office. However, the final book can be assembled using any desktop publishing program and copying facilities.

8. This idea would work well with any aspect of the students' cultures: poetry, recipes, fashion, and so forth.

Appendix: Sample Folktales

• - 선녀와 나무꾼 - •

아주 먼 옛날, 홀로 외로이 사는 젊은 나무꾼이 있었다. 그는 항상 나무를 팔아서 돈을 모으곤 했었다. 예전과 다름없이 나무를 베고 있는데 작은사슴이 살려달라며 착한 나무꾼에게 애원을 하였다. 착한 이 나무꾼은 그 사슴이 너무나 가여워서 자기의 나뭇짐 뒤에 숨겨주곤 사냥꾼에게 사슴같은건 보지 않았다며 거짓말을 하게 된다.

무서운 사냥꾼이 돌아간뒤, 사슴은 그에게 고맙다는 인사말과 함께 색시감을 구하는 방법을 일러주었다. 그는 사슴이 시킨대로 그 강가에가서 선녀의 옷한벌을 훔쳤어요. 그는 옷이없어 하늘로 올라가지 못하는 그녀에게 청을 구했어요. 어렇게 선녀가 허락을 하여 둘은 함께 살았어요.

행복하게 살면서도 그녀는 항상 그 옷 입고 싶어했다. 그래서 그는 아이를 2명 가졌을때 그녀에게 그 옷을낳아주었다. 그러자 그녀 아이를 한팔씩 안고 하늘로 올라갔어요. 그는 자기가 한 행동에 대해 후회를 하며 다시 그 강가로 갔더니 사슴이 대신번쩍 그에게 방법을 알려주었어요.

그날 저녁, 그는 하늘에서 내려온 두레박으로 타고서는 올라가 사랑하는 가족들을 만났어요. 아이도 한명 더 낳고 언제까지 행복하게 살았답니다.

The Woodcutter and the Fairy
A Korean Folk Tale

A long time ago, a man who was a woodcutter lived alone. He cut down trees and sold them.

One day, a small deer came and said to him, "Please help me. If the hunters catch me, they will kill me." The woodcutter hid the deer in his hut. The hunters came to him but he didn't tell them where the deer was. The hunters went away and the deer said, "Thank you very much for helping me." The deer wanted to repay him so it told him how to find a wife.

The deer said, "Go to the river and steal the clothes of the youngest girl. She is a fairy. If she doesn't have her special clothes, she can't go back to heaven." So he went to the river and stole her clothes.

They were married and later had two children. One day the wife wanted to dress up in her special clothes. She did and she took her children and went to heaven.

The woodcutter was sad. He wanted to go to heaven too. So the deer told him how to get there.

One day he went to heaven and met his wife and his children. They lived there happily ever after.

Contributor

Judith Sharp has worked in Mexico, the Philippines, Hong Kong, and Japan. She has taught ESL at South Pasadena High School, in California, in the United States, since 1988.

Digging Poetry: A Literary, Anthropological Quest

Levels
High intermediate +; high school

Aims
Distinguish poetic voice
Discover cultural markers in poetry and universal themes
Appreciate the work of various multicultural poets
Engage in literary criticism
Work cooperatively
Use whole language techniques to write recursively from text

Activity Type
Cooperative project, practice, or application

Class Time
Several class periods

Preparation Time
Variable

Resources
Packet of teacher-selected poetry by multicultural poets for each student
Deck of playing cards
Writing notebooks

This multimodal learning adventure looks deeply at poetry as a cultural phenomenon. It involves cooperative learning tasks, engages critical thinking skills, and leads to personal response.

Procedure

1. Have each student select a card from a shuffled deck and look for the other members of his or her poetry club, namely those with the same number (or picture) card to represent all the suits (spades, hearts, diamonds, clubs).

2. Present the task to the class: Each poetry club is going on a quest and must decide on the country of origin and gender of an unidentified poet by "digging" for cultural markers in the text, whether explicit or implicit. (See Appendix A for a list of possible poets from which to choose.) Call on one student to "echo" the task, that is, repeat it aloud to check and reinforce class comprehension. Set a time limit.

3. Assign roles to the group members: facilitator, time keeper, recorder, and so forth.

4. Distribute poetry packets to the groups and tell the students to read the poems and highlight the cultural markers.

5. Tell groups to discuss their opinions to reach a group decision about the country and gender of the poet. When the groups are finished, have the facilitators report the outcomes of the group quest. As a class, discuss the outcomes reported.

6. Reveal the names and genders of the poets, countries of origin, and the historical time periods of authorship.

7. Explain to students that they will now write a personal response to one of the poems. Tell them to select a poem from the packet and choose a phrase or verse that is meaningful for them. In their writing

notebooks (or on paper) they should copy the phrase or verse and write a response or reaction.

8. Collect the notebooks and write a written response to the student entries or pair the students and have them exchange notebooks and respond in writing to their partner's entry.

Caveats and Options

1. Avoid selecting hackneyed poetry that students are already familiar with. When selecting work by a popular poet or a particular culture, aim for a poem that is not very well known yet contains cultural markers (e.g., "Desert Places" by Robert Frost, 1936).

2. Group roles can be assigned through teacher-directed clues. For example, the person with the longest thumb is the time keeper. The person who lives closest to the school is the recorder.

3. You can vary the number of poems included in the packet according to the amount of time available and student proficiency levels.

4. This lesson is excellent for use in professional development workshops or sensitivity training seminars.

5. If you write poetry or your colleagues do, you may want to include your/their work in the packet (see Appendix B).

References and Further Reading

Lathem, E.C. (Ed.). (1969). *The poetry of Robert Frost*. New York: Holt, Rinehart & Winston.

Appendix A: Poets with a Cultural Voice

Yehudah Amichai, Israel
Elizabeth Bishop, United States
Red Bone, U.S. Native American
Sandra Cisneros, U.S. Latina
Ralph Waldo Emerson, United States
Robert Frost, United States
Allen Ginsburg, United States
Seamus Heaney, Ireland
June Jordan, Jamaica
Li Young Lee, U.S. Asian American

Pablo Neruda, Chile
Jeladdin Rumi, 13th-century Persian Sufi master
Wole Soyinka, Nigeria
Wislawa Szymborska, Poland
Rabindranath Tagore, India
Piri Thomas, Mexico
Derek Walcott, West Indies/Caribbean
Alice Walker, United States

Appendix B: Sample Poem

Marathon

by Judith Rose

I'm a long distance runner on the track of life
Seasoned athlete of my profession
Father Time brandishes his hourglass before my tired eyes
His sickle whistles as he swings another minute off my future.

Run, Girl
Just Run...

Here at Midway days are stacked as neatly as the desks of German bankers
Plotted out like shopping lists and tables for the time
Breathlessly I race to beat the Old Man's sickle
To fill the noted order for each second and each sand.

Run, Girl
Just Run...

The ticking of the clock is echoed in the beating of my soul
A flaming soul that yearns to burn its brand on Mother Earth
May this breathless sprinter not neglect along the course
To pause sometime to see the glisten of the stardust and the sand.

Contributor

Judith Rose has taught ESL for more than 10 years at the high school and community college levels in New York, in the United States.

Buddy Journals Build Relationships and Literacy

Levels
Beginning–intermediate

Aims
Build peer relationships
and friendships
Develop literacy and
build writing fluency
Develop understanding
and respect for other
cultures and countries

Activity Type
Cooperative project

Class Time
10–15 minutes

Preparation Time
20–30 minutes to
introduce
5–10 minutes to model
and share entries later

Resources
Spiral notebooks, loose-
leaf binders, or journals
made by stapling
wallpaper covers to
sheets of lined paper
Pens, pencils, felt-tip
markers

In buddy journals, when ESL and native-English-speaking students are matched to write back and forth, they become friends as they build literacy and writing fluency. Students have an audience other than the teacher as they practice literacy skills and write to a peer about what is important to them.

Procedure

1. Identify the scope of buddy journals. Decide whether to make them a project within the classroom or a collaborative venture with two classes, either at the same grade level or across grade levels.

2. Introduce buddy journals and identify objectives together. Help students understand the rationale for buddy journals so they are committed. Inform parents so they understand this informal, personal writing is not your complete writing program, but an important part that is a precursor and bridge to academic writing.

3. Use student ideas to create a list of topics and rules. Post these on a bulletin board or have students put copies in their journals. Keeping a list of ideas close at hand gives hesitant students ready access to topics they can explore and a quick reminder of rules to follow.

4. Match students. Do this voluntarily, randomly, or according to grade level, gender, interests, strengths, needs, reading and writing performance, or personalities, depending on your particular students and classroom situation. Be sensitive to potential incompatibility between buddies and flexible in changing the pairs.

5. Model appropriate content and form for entries. First, brainstorm topics for buddy journals with students. Hobbies, family, pets, favorites (e.g., books, foods, TV shows, sports), dreams, wishes,

opinions of current events, and other such ideas make good topics. Create model entries and share them with students, then create entries with students using their input and suggestions. Keep exemplars from one year to the next to share with students. (See Appendix.)

6. Have students decorate and personalize notebooks or journal covers with their names and pictures since this builds ownership.

7. Make time for regular journal writing. Set aside 10-15 minutes daily or every other day to establish the habit of journal writing. It is most successful when it becomes part of the daily routine (e.g., first thing in the morning, after lunch or recess, at the end of each day).

8. Exchange journals. This may be done daily, every other day, or weekly depending on interest and schedules. When students write often, their interest remains high.

9. Monitor journals frequently. Read entries on a regular basis to assess writing performance and plan for small group instruction in specific writing skills. Regular monitoring allows you to identify inappropriate content or relationships that are not working so you can deal with these problems.

10. Plan time for students to socialize together occasionally. Maintain enthusiasm and enrich peer relationships by allowing buddies to spend time interacting together at lunch, recess, or a special time set aside for reading entries to each other, talking, or playing games.

11. Reevaluate regularly and make changes as necessary. Writing to the same buddy for 4-6 weeks may be long enough for some students who will need a change and be ready to write to someone new.

Caveats and Options

1. Ask one group of students to begin writing, then pass the journals to another group of students who can write back. This allows one conversation to occur between buddies and may be preferable if students are not fluent writers. At the conclusion there is only one journal for one buddy to keep, although a copy could be made for the other. The alternate method is for both buddies to begin a journal and then exchange each. This permits two separate conver-

sations simultaneously between buddies. At the end of this arrangement, each buddy has a journal to keep.

2. Use this activity in science, math, or social studies classes as a way to share new knowledge, pose questions, and answer each other's queries.

3. Encourage drawing and labeling pictures to reinforce vocabulary.

4. Alternate with other types of journals, such as home-school, literature response, dialogue, or learning logs.

5. Stop journals altogether for a time if interest wanes.

References and Further Reading

Bromley, K. (1995). Buddy journals for ESL and native-English-speaking students. *TESOL Journal, 4* (3), 7–11.

Bromley, K. (1993). *Journaling: Engagements in reading, writing, and thinking.* New York: Scholastic.

Bromley, K. (1989). Buddy journals make the reading-writing connection. *The Reading Teacher, 43,* 122–129.

Foster, L. A. (1989). Breaking down racial isolation. *Educational Leadership, 47,* 76–77.

Appendix: Sample Entries

Hi Autumn Howareyo
Doyou like dog
I like.littledogs?
Autumn Do you like rabbits
I like small white rabbits.
Autumn Doyou like to read books?
I like books about birds.

Vu

Dear Vu,
yes i do like dogs. I
like a germing shepard
What is your favorite
food. Mine is pizza from
Puggies and pizza
hut.
sincerly autumn

Drawing and journal entry by Vu, 10, and response by Autumn. Used with permission.

Dear Amanda,

I live at 809 Burbank Avenue. My phone number is 798-7844. (You can call me any time) My favorite color is aqua. I have 5 people (including me.) My hobbie is running, jumping, climbing, and reading. Here is a map

Emily

Dear Emily,
My number is 797-4488 you can call any time. my favorite color is Purple. My brother has to have sargery. Pinky Promise you won't tell. I think your nice and very pretty. I like you a lot.
Here is a map

Emily, an ESL student, provides Amanda, a native-English-speaking student, with a fluent model to imitate. Used with permission.

Contributor

Karen Bromley is a professor at Binghamton University, State University of New York, in the United States, where she teaches courses in literacy, language arts, and children's literature.

Mock Trial

Levels
Intermediate +

Aims
Practice speaking,
listening, and critical
thinking

Activity Type
Cooperative project or
application

Class Time
$1^{1}/_{2}$–2 hours

Preparation Time
None

Resources
None

In this open-ended activity, students start with a simple list of facts about a crime and a suspect and build versions of the events through discussion and role-play. The verdict depends on how well each side is able to put together a case.

Procedure

1. Ask the class to choose a setting and a brief list of facts about a crime. For example, "The victim, John, was seen in a restaurant with the suspect. They left together and were later seen at a night club having an argument. Later John's dead body was found in his car." The facts should act as a framework; therefore, they should be simple, yet general, so that each side can fill in details that fit the established parameters.

2. As needed, discuss criminal trials and the U.S. judicial system to activate background schema and build anticipation.

3. Have students take roles. Students with strong language skills should play the part of the defense and prosecuting attorneys. Each attorney will work with three witnesses, so there will be a total of six witnesses. The defense attorney also will work with the defendant. Remaining students will play judge, jury, and reporters, depending on the size of the class.

4. Send the two attorneys and their groups (witnesses, defendant) to different corners of the room and give them time to prepare cases based on the list of "facts" developed earlier. Each side must negotiate a story that will help win the case and that sticks with the established facts. The sides do not communicate with each other. For the crime described above, for example, the defense might say that the victim

was drinking because he was upset about some money he had borrowed from a bad guy. The defendant was trying to control John's drinking and was acting in his best interests. The prosecution might counter that the bartender heard the defendant threatening John. Both sides fit the story, but neither side knew what the other would say. The outcome will be based mainly on the ability of the attorneys and witnesses to be consistent and convincing regarding their respective cases. Students can be very creative in putting together their cases as long as they are not limited by too many details from the start.

5. While the two sides are conferring, discuss the format for the trial with the judge and jury. Instruct members of the press to prepare a news bulletin about the case.

6. Hold the trial. Give the judge the responsibility for keeping order in the court. As in most trials, the prosecuting attorney should call witnesses to the stand first; the defense attorney, second. Each attorney may cross-examine the other's witnesses to look for discrepancies.

7. After all witnesses have spoken, and the defendant has told his or her side (if desired), have the lawyers make closing statements. Have the jury meet and then declare a verdict.

8. The reporters may choose to ask questions of the people involved after the verdict has been issued. They then summarize the events and make a report for "the evening news."

Caveats and Options

1. This activity is an ideal follow-up to a reading on a criminal case or on the justice system.

2. If students are not familiar with courtroom scenes, discuss them and introduce key vocabulary, such as judge, jury, jury box, attorney, lawyer, witness, defense, prosecute, victim, suspect, and so on. If desired, show video clips of courtroom scenes from film or television.

3. The first time this activity is presented, you may want to plan the crime and facts in advance to model that step for the students.

4. Some students may be designated newspaper reporters and have to write an article about the trial for publication.

5. This activity can be adapted for civil cases.

Contributor

Alice Savage teaches at Houston Community College and is working toward a MAT at the School for International Training, in Vermont, in the United States.

Part VI: Assessment, Review, and Language Games

Editor's Note

The activities in this section offer exciting ways for students to review what they have learned and for teachers to check student knowledge. Several activities are geared to student self-evaluation. The first activity helps students set and reflect on learning goals over the course of a quarter, semester, or school year. The remaining activities are designed in a gamelike fashion and can be conducted near the end of a class period for a change of pace or an informal assessment. Some activities focus on vocabulary; others, on grammar; still others, on content.

How Are You Doing? Using Student Progress Journals for Self-Assessment

Levels
Intermediate; middle school

Aims
Become familiar with different strategies for success
Think about and evaluate progress toward meeting a goal
Become more responsible for learning
Practice writing

Activity Type
Assessment or motivation

Class Time
One or two 40-minute periods, biweekly

Preparation Time
15–30 minutes, biweekly, for a class of about 25

Resources
Motivational sayings
Assessment questions
Student notebooks or journals

Students select learning goals, develop action plans, and record their progress in journals biweekly during a marking period. Although the focus here is on developing language skills, this approach will contribute to the students' overall education.

Procedure

Part I: Developing an Action Plan

1. Select an appropriate motivational saying and write it on the board. (See Appendix A.)
2. Ask students to write a response to the saying in a designated section of their notebook or in a journal book. Explain that this will be their progress journal and that they will be writing in it every 2 weeks to help them become better students.
3. After a few minutes, ask for volunteers to read their responses to the class.
4. Facilitate a class discussion about the relationship between the students' journal responses and the need for effort to be successful in school.
5. Ask the students what aspect of achievement they would like to improve in this class. Elicit ideas from a number of students and record the ideas on the board in the form of a goal. (See samples in Appendix B.) Writing the goals down provides modeling for others to think of their own goals.
6. Review each goal and ask students what they would need to do to achieve that goal. List their strategies as in Appendix B. This is a brainstorming activity. The more varied the ideas, the better.

7. Explain that each student is going to set a goal for the current marking period. Discuss making goals achievable and realistic. Have the students record their goal in their progress journal:

     I would like to _____.

8. Ask students to select or think of three or more strategies they will use to achieve their goal for the marking period. Have them record these strategies in their journals:

     To achieve my goal, I will:
     1. _____
     2. _____
     3. _____

   This becomes their action plan.

9. Have each student explain his or her goal and strategies to you while the rest of the class listens. This activity allows students to learn from each other and is especially helpful to students having difficulty thinking of goals or strategies. Record the goals and strategies as in Appendix B, preferably on chart paper, and keep as a visual reminder for both the students and yourself.

Part II: Student Assessment of Their Action Plan
(2 weeks later, and then biweekly)

1. Explain that you are going to write some questions for the class to help them think about their progress. (Choose several from the samples in Appendix C.) The students should respond in their progress journals. (Add or delete questions for subsequent lessons as appropriate.)

2. Repeat Steps 1–3 in the development section above.

3. Ask students to make a connection between the saying you have chosen for the lesson and their progress toward meeting their goal so far.

4. Collect the progress journals. Read and write a response to each.

5. Select meaningful passages to read to the class when you return the journals to validate the students' ideas and raise awareness. This validation will encourage students to write more reflectively the next time.

6. Use the information in the journals to tailor instruction to individual students' needs.

Caveats and Options

1. Distribute certificates to students who reach their goals.
2. You may want to encourage students to set goals for other classes.
3. Most students initially set goals related to grades, such as tests or report cards. Some students will be able to achieve those goals, however there tends to be a leveling off. Consequently, it is important to encourage students to develop goals related to skills in addition to grade achievement in order to avoid discouragement. Those students who are already achieving at a high level can set a goal to maintain that high level, or work on certain areas of weakness.
4. Before a test or other graded assignments, students could develop a specific action plan for that graded assignment. After they receive their grade, they should assess the effectiveness of their action plan.
5. Repeat this process each marking period throughout the semester or year to allow students flexibility in experimenting with new goals and new strategies. Repetition enhances learning.

References and Further Reading

Sharkey, J. (1994–1995). Helping students become better learners. *TESOL Journal, 4* (2), 18–22.

The Efficiency Institute, Inc. (1987). *The efficiency seminar for educators.* Lexington, KY: Author.

Appendix A: Examples of Motivational Sayings

1. If you do what you always did, you will get what you always got.
2. Insanity is doing the same thing over and over and expecting different results.
3. Failure is the opportunity to begin again differently.
4. Genius is 1% inspiration and 99% perspiration.
5. Smart is not something you are; smart is something you get.
6. Confidence is the belief that you can control your outcome.
7. Teachers open the door, but only you can decide to walk through it.

Appendix B: Examples of Action Plan

Goals

I would like to:

1. raise my grade
2. maintain my grade of 90

3. participate more

4. improve my pronunciation

5. raise my test grades

6. speak more English

Strategies

To achieve my goal, I will:

1. do all my homework
2. continue studying, doing my homework, and participating
3. sit in front; pay attention, raise my hand
4. practice at home; listen to the radio
5. review my class notes every night; study 15 minutes longer before a test
6. speak to my friends in English; make telephone calls in English

Appendix C: Sample Questions for Self-Assessment

1. What is your goal?
2. What are you doing to reach your goal?
3. Describe any problems you are having with your action plan.
4. What is going well for you?
5. How do you feel about your effort?
6. What do you need to do differently?
7. Have you reached your goal? Explain.
8. Is your goal realistic for you? Explain why.
9. How are you doing in this class in terms of tests, homework, classwork, projects, and such?
10. What grade do you expect to earn this marking period? Why?
11. Which of the following areas of your learning are you pleased with, and which ones would you like to improve: speaking, pronunciation, listening, writing, reading, vocabulary? Explain.

Contributor

Jane Berkowicz teaches ESL and is the ESL coordinator at Theodore Roosevelt High School, in New York, in the United States. During the summer of 1994, she trained Ukrainian EFL teachers in Kiev.

Focus!!

Levels
Any; high school

Aims
Focus energy and
concentrate at the
beginning or end of
class
Develop listening,
concentration, and
memory skills

Activity Type
Review or motivation

Class Time
5-10 minutes

Preparation Time
5 minutes

Resources
Chalkboard or overhead
projector
Grid with numbers

Focus is a verbal version of the matching card game called Concentration. It is an ideal warm-up or review. It requires concentration and listening, but is not difficult from a language production point of view, making it ideal for mixed-level classes.

Procedure

1. To prepare, think of 10 questions and their answers. These can be review or preview items, or just trivia, but they should not be difficult. The student energy in this activity is to be spent on concentration, not on coming up with the correct answer. Assign questions and answers random numbers 1–20 (see Appendix A).
2. Have students form two teams.
3. The first player from the first team chooses one number from the grid. Repeat the number, and read aloud the question or answer that corresponds. Then, have the same student pick another number. Repeat that number and read the question or answer that corresponds. If the two numbers picked represent a matching question and answer, that student's team will get one point. (This is unlikely at the start of the game.)
4. The first player from the opposing team then picks one number and then a second, trying to match a question and answer. Some students may not understand how the game works at first, but eventually they will catch on that the trick is not to know the answer to the question, but to know the numbers of the matching questions and answers. With that, they will realize that in order to know how to match them, they need to pay attention even when it is not their turn. Even so, it may take time before students start making successful matches.

5. As correct matches are made, cross the numbers out on the grid. The team that successfully makes a match wins a point. With increasingly fewer options, the game becomes easier as it progresses, making it ideal for a warm-up activity in those classes that often get late-comers in the first few minutes.

Caveats and Options

1. Insist that each student in the group have a turn to select numbers. Other group members can help with their idea of what the correct answer is, but the person whose turn it is must make the choice.
2. I have found that sometimes the skills needed to be successful at this activity are possessed by students who do not necessarily have the best language skills. The game gives these students a much needed chance to feel successful in the language classroom.
3. The questions and answers can be scribbled down in order and then assigned random numbers. Because the teacher is the only one to see the sheet, it does not need to be neatly typed and can be easily customized to a class.
4. Each student can be asked to submit one or two easy questions and answers for a review, and these can be made into a list for the next day's warm-up.
5. If a shorter activity is desired, use only 12 or 16 squares in the grid.

Appendix A: Sample Questions and Answers

1. What is a baby cow called?
2. Atlanta
3. What is the first name of Bill Clinton's wife?
4. A piglet
5. What color is snow?
6. October
7. In what month is Christmas?
8. December
9. A calf
10. What city hosted the 1996 Summer Olympics?
11. Halloween

12. In what city is the Statue of Liberty found?
13. Hillary
14. What is a baby pig called?
15. New York City
16. What color is a carrot?
17. White
18. In what month is Halloween?
19. Orange
20. What is the name of a U.S. holiday in October?

Appendix B: Sample Grid

1	2	3	4	5
6	7	8	9	10
11	12	13	14	15
16	17	18	19	20

Contributor

Elizabeth Bigler has taught English and ESL in academic, adult, and refugee programs, in Georgia, in the United States, and in Japan. She has an MS in applied linguistics/ESL from Georgia State University.

Reverse Jeopardy

Levels
Any

Aims
Review information
Self-evaluate
Practice reading and
speaking

Activity Type
Review or practice

Class Time
30–40 minutes

Preparation Time
30 minutes

Resources
Chalkboard or poster
paper
Reverse Jeopardy grid

Through this game, students can review information taught in class, ranging from grammar items to vocabulary to content material. Students select questions according to topic and level of difficulty in order to gain points for their team.

Procedure

1. Before class, prepare the reverse jeopardy grid, five columns by five rows. Select category topics for the columns, such as: Verb Tenses, Science Vocabulary, Music, Community Services, Fairy Tales. These categories are placed at the top of the columns. The rows represent money. The boxes in the first row are worth $100; in the second row, $200; in the third, $300; the fourth, $400; and the fifth, $500. (See sample grid in Appendix.)

2. Plan five questions for each topic; the first question should be the easiest, the fifth the most difficult. The questions will be worth $100 to $500, respectively. For example, in the category Verb Tenses, questions can range from: "What is the past tense of *to talk*?" to "What is the tense of the verb *to be* in the following sentence: *If I _____ happy, I would dance*?" For the category Science Vocabulary, questions could range from: "Name a flower." to "What is the name of the tube inside plants that transports water?" In general, the questions can refer to definitions, synonyms, story characters, plot events, famous people, field trips, and so forth.

3. The grid can be drawn on the blackboard or poster paper before class with the questions written in the boxes. The boxes could be covered with pieces of paper on which the money amounts are written. When the students play the game, the paper is removed from the questions

that are selected. The teacher reads the questions aloud while the students read along silently.

4. During class, explain to the students how the game is played. It is a modified version of the television game show. Divide the class into two teams and line them up facing the board. The first student on Team A chooses any question, saying, for example, "Fairy Tales for $100." If he or she answers correctly, Team A gets the $100 added to its score and the first student moves to the back of the line. The next student from Team A gets to choose another question and play continues. If the first student does not answer correctly, Team A loses $100 and Team B has the option to answer. Students may consult as a team for 30 seconds. If they answer correctly, they get the $100. Then the first student on Team B chooses a question. If Team B does not answer Team A's question correctly, there is no penalty. The game goes on with the first student of Team B selecting a question.

5. Play continues until all the questions are selected and answered or until the class period ends. The team with the highest score wins.

Caveats and Options

1. All questions should have one answer. For example, do not ask students to name three types of something. However, if a student provides a reasonable answer that is different from the one you intended, you should accept it.

2. When a team member selects a question, only he or she may answer it. To prevent team members from shouting out the answers, you may want to impose a penalty, such as a $25 deduction for each answer called out of turn.

3. You may want to plan a prize for the winning team. A homework pass, good for one night free from doing homework, or a snack, are possibilities.

4. Sometimes, teams decide to ask only for the questions which will garner the largest sums of money. Try to encourage students to choose questions within their ability range.

5. If neither team answers a question correctly, you can provide the answer or save the question until the end of the game and use it as a bonus question or to resolve a tie.

6. To practice listening comprehension skills, you may want to read the questions aloud to the students without showing them the written question.

7. As the class becomes more accustomed to this game, you may want to introduce regular Jeopardy. In this situation, students are given the answer and need to make up a correct question. This is a good skill for the students to practice; however, it may be necessary at first to remind them to use question forms as they respond.

Appendix: Reverse Jeopardy Grid Setup

Verb Tenses	Science Vocab.	Music	Comm. Services	Fairy Tales
$100	$100	$100	$100	$100
$200	$200	$200	$200	$200
$300	$300	$300	$300	$300
$400	$400	$400	$400	$400
$500	$500	$500	$500	$500

Reverse Jeopardy Grid (with sample questions revealed during play)

Verb Tenses	Science Vocab.	Music	Comm. Services	Fairy Tales
What is the past tense of *to talk?*	Name a flower.	$100	What is the telephone number for emergencies?	$100
$200	$200	What is the national anthem of the United States?	$200	$200
$300	$300	$300	$300	$300
$400	$400	$400	$400	Name the fairy tale with a goose that lays golden eggs.
What is the tense of *to be* in this sentence?: *If I _____ happy, I would dance.*	What is the name of the tube that transports water inside plants?	$500	$500	$500

Contributor

Deborah Short conducts research at the Center for Applied Linguistics, in Washington, DC, in the United States, and directs the ESL Standards and Assessment Project for TESOL.

Grammar Dice

Levels
Beginning

Aims
Manipulate language
mechanics (grammatical
forms, vocabulary,
pronunciation)

Class Time
15–20 minutes

Preparation Time
Up to 1 hour

Resources
Approximately 100
3-in. x 5-in. cards
(depending on class
size)
Several sets of small
pictures (if possible,
taken from a basal text)
Several dice
Masking tape and
marker

Grammar Dice gives students practice in manipulating a target grammatical structure. Students use previously studied vocabulary (mounted on cards) and dice to create new sentences in small groups.

Procedure

1. To develop the material:
   - Select a grammar topic to practice or review (e.g., verb tense).
   - Photocopy 5–10 small (2-in. x 2-in.) pictures that can be described using vocabulary that students already know (e.g., pictures of people doing some action like going to a movie or playing soccer). A basal or beginning-level text will be a good source of picture cues; otherwise, you can make simple line drawings. Plan to divide your students into small groups and make one set of pictures per group.
   - Cut out and mount the pictures on the 3-in. x 5-in. cards. Bind each complete set with a rubber band.
   - Wrap dice in masking tape. Label each die face with a different subject (e.g., *I, Mary, Victor, Bob & Amy*) or verb tense cue word (e.g., *now, every day, yesterday*). Prepare one die per group.
2. To play the game, put students in groups of three or four. Give each group one set of cards and one die.
3. Demonstrate how to play by holding up a card. Ask the class to describe the picture to check their vocabulary (e.g., *go to the movies*). Roll one die and read what is written on the die face aloud (e.g., *yesterday*). Ask someone to make a sentence (e.g., *Yesterday I went to the movies.*). Roll the die several times using the same cue card and make more sentences.
4. Tell students to proceed in the same way in their groups.

Caveats and Options

1. This activity is very useful in teaching languages with extensive verb conjugations (e.g., Spanish). To make it livelier in English, cue cards could include other lexical groups, such as phrasal verbs.
2. A variation would be to use two dice per group, one for the subject and the other for the tense.
3. More advanced students could try to make very long sentences using prepositional phrases or subordinate clauses (Yesterday I went to the movies with my brother.) or "true" sentences (*Yesterday I did not go to the movies, but Sam did.*).
4. Difficult vocabulary can be reinforced by writing word prompts on the back of each picture card. In this way, one student in the group can hold up the card to show the picture to the others· and if necessary, teach unknown or forgotten vocabulary.
5. For non-artists or teachers with limited preparation time, use word cues instead of picture cues (e.g., *go/movies*).
6. Other sources for pictures are newspaper and advertisement circulars.

References and Further Reading

Moran, P. *Lexicarry.* Brattleboro, VT: Pro Lingua Associates.

Wright, A. (1995). *1,000+ pictures for teachers to copy.* Reading MA: Addison-Wesley Longman.

Contributor

Dennis Bricault is registrar, director of ESL Programs, and instructor in Spanish at North Park University, in Illinois, in the United States. He has also worked as a teacher and administrator in Spain and Hungary.

Sentence Poker

This sentence-making game gives learners an opportunity to work on grammatical structures in a nonthreatening and enjoyable format. An element of chance and turn taking precludes lower level students from being left out, while the competitive nature of the game keeps all participants motivated and focused on making correct sentences.

Procedure

1. Write several sets of statements, negations, and yes/no questions using interesting verbs and prepositional phrases. For example: *Marty dances with bugs in his house. Does Leah boil shrimp for dinner? I surprise my friends at parties. Jeremy does not snore in his sleep.*

2. Transfer the sentences onto index cards. Put one word or prepositional phrase on each card. For example, "Marty" would go on one card, "dances" would go on another, but "with bugs" or "in his house" would go on other cards. (The prepositional phrases add humor and make the game more challenging.) Make several decks. They need not all include the same words and phrases.

3. Ask whether any students know how to play poker. Explain that they are going to play a card game that people play in Las Vegas. If you would like to use poker chips, distribute the chips at this time.

4. Model the game with a volunteer. Each puts a chip in a central location, if you decide to use chips. Deal five cards to each. The volunteer may look at the cards and see if he or she can put together a sentence from the words. The volunteer may not show the cards to anyone else. During his or her turn, the player may exchange any number of cards with the dealer one time, up to all five, or the player may choose not to exchange any. Next, the dealer looks at his or her cards and exchanges any cards that he or she cannot use. When both

303

players have exchanged cards, they may bet additional chips. Then, both show their sentences, made from as many cards as possible. The player with the longest correct sentence is the winner and can collect the chips, if used.

5. After answering any questions that arise, break students into small groups. Designate stronger students to be dealers and give each group a deck of cards.

6. Facilitate and mediate while the students play.

Caveats and Options

1. It is not necessary to use all the cards to win. *Maria has bugs* can win, if it is the longest sentence in the group. Also, silly sentences, such as, *I want bugs for dinner,* are acceptable.

2. Sentence Poker is an ideal way to review for a test. Students manipulate words and phrases, and they discuss meaning and form among themselves in an informal setting. The teacher can observe and get indirect feedback on how well students understand the grammar structures.

3. Sentence Poker can be adapted to work with any sentence structure that is new to students. When adapting, however, keep the variety of possible structures limited or players may have difficulty forming sentences. Present tense works well because there is an appropriate number of possible combinations and the odds that every student will have at least a short sentence are favorable.

4. Other options are to have students write the sentences or make the cards themselves.

5. Some teachers or students may feel uncomfortable with the gambling aspect of sentence poker. The game works just as well without betting.

Contributor

Alice Savage teaches at Houston Community College and is working toward a MAT at the School for International Training, in Vermont, in the United States.

Auction

Levels
Intermediate +; high
school

Aims
Identify and correct
grammar problems in
own written sentences

Activity Type
Review or application

Class Time
15–30 minutes

Preparation Time
Variable

Resources
Overhead projector and
transparencies
Sentences from students'
homework
Play money

This is an interactive activity that allows students to review the grammar structures they have studied and apply them to writing.

Procedure

1. The object of this game is for small groups of students to "buy" correct sentences. Before class or before the activity, write 8–10 sentences that you have collected from students' homework or journals in advance, mixing up correct with incorrect sentences. Display them on an overhead transparency or blackboard.

2. Explain to students how an auction works. Then divide the students into small groups and have each group determine among themselves which sentences are correct and which are incorrect. The group should also determine how the incorrect sentence would be corrected. Give each group an equal amount of money (e.g., $500 in play money) with which to bid. Now you are ready to begin.

3. As the auctioneer, try to persuade students to buy each sentence as it comes up. For example, the teacher could say, "Here's Sentence 1. I'll start the bidding at $10. Which group wants to buy this beautiful sentence? Going once! Going twice . . . Oh, Group 2 just bid $10. Will anyone give me $20?"

4. When the sentence has finally been sold and the money has been collected, tell everyone whether or not the sentence is correct. If the sentence is incorrect, ask one of the groups that did not buy the sentence to identify the error and correct the sentence. The auction continues until all sentences have been sold. The team with the most correct sentences at the end wins.

Caveats and Options

1. Make sure that students understand what an auction is. Also make sure that they know they will lose money if they buy incorrect sentences.
2. You could vary the game by giving a certain sum of money to the group that corrects an incorrect sentence.

References and Further Reading

Jones, D., & Nelson Thompson, D. (1995). Four enjoyable test review activities. *TESOL Journal, 5* (1), 40-41.

Contributors

Diana Thompson Nelson is a teacher at CELOP at Boston University, Massachusetts in the United States. She received her MA in TESL in August 1995. Dawnell Jones, who holds an MA in TESL, is a faculty member at the English Language Center at Brigham Young University, Utah, in the United States.

Classroom Feud

Levels
Beginning-intermediate

Aims
Review vocabulary
Reinforce previously
taught material
Practice speaking and
listening

Activity Type
Assessment or review

Class Time
10-15 minutes

Preparation Time
5-20 minutes

Resources
Object for students to
grab (e.g., ball, pen,
eraser)
Timer or watch

Caveats and Options

This activity is a quick, easy, and enjoyable way to review material and prepare students for an upcoming exam. The game enables teachers to assess how well the students have mastered the material presented in class.

Procedure

1. Prepare a list of prompts or questions pertaining to review material in advance. For example, if the topic is the environment, sample prompts could be:
   - Give an example of air pollution.
   - Name two things you can recycle.
2. Divide students into two teams. Ask a representative from each team to come to the front of the classroom and stand on either side of the desk. Place an object, such as a ball or pen, on the desk. Instruct the students that when they know the answer to the question, they should grab the object from the middle of the desk and then answer the question.
3. Ask the questions one at a time. The first student to grab the object must give the correct answer within 5 seconds or the turn goes to the other team. If the person who grabbed the object does not answer or gives an incorrect answer, the other team's representative can consult with the rest of the team before answering the question. The team that answers correctly receives one point.

1. Be sure to explain the instructions clearly and inform students that if the team representative who first grabs the object does not know the correct answer, the other team members may not shout out the answer.

2. This activity may be done with students writing the questions for the teacher to read. (This will reduce teacher preparation time.) However, the teacher must be careful not to ask any student a question that student has written.

References and Further Reading

Jones, D., & Nelson Thompson, D. (1995). Four enjoyable test review activities. *TESOL Journal, 5* (1), 40–41.

Contributors

Diana Thompson Nelson is a teacher at CELOP at Boston University, Massachusetts, in the United States. She received her MA in TESL in August 1995. Dawnell Jones, who has an MA in TESL, is a faculty member at the English Language Center at Brigham Young University, Utah, in the United States.

Row Recall and Review

Levels
Beginning-intermediate

Aims
Review vocabulary
Use vocabulary to
describe objects
Practice speaking and
listening

Activity Type
Assessment or review

Class Time
10-20 minutes

Preparation Time
10 minutes

Resources
Familiar objects related
to a topic that students
know about (e.g., fruit:
banana, apple, orange,
mango, kiwi)

This is a communicative activity that encourages participation of all students and gives them opportunities to interact with other members of the class.

Procedure

1. Arrange the desks in two rows that face each other. Each desktop should be touching the desktop immediately in front of it. If possible, leave space on the left and right sides of the paired desks.
2. Announce a topic, such as school supplies or occupations. Stand behind one row and hold up an object, word, or phrase that is related to the topic. For beginning levels, you may want to bring the actual objects related to the topic (e.g., notebook, pen, eraser). For more advanced levels, you can write the word on a piece of paper (e.g., doctor, plumber). Students in the row facing the teacher must explain the object, word, or phrase to the student sitting directly in front of them. This student then tries to guess what the word is.
3. The teacher then stands behind the other row and repeats this action. After students have guessed two or three words, students in one row should rotate down one seat to allow each of them to have various partners.

Caveats and Options

1. We have found this activity is most productive if students are given a guideline to follow. For example, if students are describing words pertaining to sports, prior to doing this activity the teacher could write questions on the board such as the following: Where is it played? Is it a team or an individual sport? What equipment is used?

This provides an outline for students to follow when they are describing the word to their partner.

2. This activity could also be used in a reading class to reinforce what the students have read. For example, the names of the main characters, as well as key vocabulary words, could be used as items for students to guess.

References and Further Reading

Jones, D., & Nelson Thompson, D. (1995). Four enjoyable test review activities. *TESOL Journal, 5* (1), 40–41.

Contributors

Diana Thompson Nelson is a teacher at CELOP at Boston University, Massachusetts, in the United States. Dawnell Jones, who has an MA in TESL, is a faculty member at the English Language Center at Brigham Young University, Utah, in the United States.

Tongue-Tied

Levels
Any

Aims
Review vocabulary
Practice speaking and
listening
Use English creatively

Activity Type
Assessment or review

Class Time
5-15 minutes

Preparation Time
20 minutes

Resources
Index cards or slips of
paper with words

This activity is a takeoff from the game Taboo and is especially effective for encouraging students to use English creatively as they describe target vocabulary words.

Procedure

1. Make sets of paired cards. Select one vocabulary category per set. Write the category (e.g., kitchen) at the top of each card. Write four or five vocabulary words pertaining to the category on one of the cards, and four or five different words on the other (see Appendix).
2. Then, pair the students and give each partner a card from the set. The cards will have the same topic heading but different words under it.
3. One student describes the first word on his or her card while the other student tries to guess it. To help the partner guess the word, a student may define the word or describe how it is used. For example, a student with the word *microwave* on his or her card might say, "This is used to heat up your food. You can cook your food quickly in this item that is shaped like a box." After the other student guesses correctly, he or she gives clues for the first word on his or her card. The game continues until all words on both cards have been guessed correctly.

Caveats and Options

1. Make sure students know the vocabulary words before they play and counsel them not to use gestures.
2. You may make all sets of cards with the same category or different sets with different categories.
3. For a variation of this activity, write only one word per card. Form sets with an equal number of cards and give them to the pairs, who turn

the cards face-down on their desks. At a given signal, the partners begin going through the stack of cards, taking turns describing the key words while the other person guesses. The first pair to finish the stack of cards wins.

References and Further Reading

Jones, D., & Nelson Thompson, D. (1995). Four enjoyable test review activities. *TESOL Journal, 5* (1), 40–41.

Appendix: Sample Cards

Card A:

| KITCHEN |
| stove |
| sink |
| cupboards |
| refrigerator |

Card B:

| KITCHEN |
| microwave |
| dishwasher |
| oven |
| plates |

Contributors

Diana Thompson Nelson is a teacher at CELOP at Boston University, Massachusetts, in the United States. She received her MA in TESL in August 1995. Dawnell Jones, who has an MA in TESL, is a faculty member at the English Language Center at Brigham Young University, Utah, in the United States.

Also available from TESOL

New Ways in Teaching Vocabulary
Paul Nation, Editor

New Ways in Teaching Writing
Ronald V. White, Editor

New Ways in Teaching Young Children
Linda Schinke-Llano and Rebecca Rauff, Editors

New Ways of Classroom Assessment
J. D. Brown, Editor

New Ways of Using Computers in Language Teaching
Tim Boswood, Editor

New Ways of Using Drama and Literature in Language Teaching
Valerie Whiteson, Editor

Reading and Writing in More Than One Language:
Lessons for Teachers
Elizabeth Franklin, Editor

For more information, contact

Teachers of English to Speakers of Other Languages, Inc.
1600 Cameron Street, Suite 300
Alexandria, Virginia 22314 USA
Tel. 703-836-0774 • Fax 703-836-7864
e-mail publ@tesol.edu
http://www.tesol.edu/